Steam Narrow Boat
'PRESIDENT'

The First Hundred Years

Compiled by Neil Ratcliffe
on behalf of The Friends of President

Published by Black Country Museum Trust Ltd
Tipton Road, Dudley, DY1 4SQ
www.bclm.co.uk

i

Edition published – 2009

Black Country Museum Trust Ltd
Tipton Road, Dudley, DY1 4SQ

ISBN 978-0-9562031-0-6

Printed by:
D.A.R. Printing Ltd, 4 Redhill Close, Thurmaston, Leics, LE4 8FU
(0116 260 3072)

Contents

Page

Acknowledgements

I would like to thank the following for all their help in the production of this book.

Malcolm Braine and Nicholas Bostock for rescuing and restoring the boat back in the 1970s, and for providing more information on their involvement once the plans for the book were made known.

Richard Thomas for all the research that he has done into the history of the boat, and for being the main proof reader. Other members of the committee for their time in proof reading, especially Dave Stott for the technical aspects of the engine and boiler.

All of the people who have provided the photographs, individually acknowledged, that are used throughout the book, apologies to anybody whose images didn't make the final version.

Finally, the Black Country Living Museum, including David McDougall and Nigel Jackson, and all past and present members of Friends of President who have kept the boat maintained and moving around the waterways system, and for creating the written and photographic records that have enabled this book to be compiled.

Front Cover: President & Kildare at the top of Farmers Bridge locks in 2004. (Photo: B.Empsall)
Rear Cover: The boats on their home mooring at the Black Country Living Museum, 1998. (Photo: R.& J. Spencer)

INTRODUCTION

It is sometimes said that one of the advantages of running somewhere like the Black Country Living Museum is that you get the opportunity to play with all the various exhibits and objects in the collections. It is sometimes true. At Beamish I had the rare experience of trying to get a 100 ton Ruston Bucyrus steam shovel to work. It had a loco type boiler and three steam engines, one to drive, one to slew and one to work the jib; and like all good steam engines you needed to talk to it to get it to work best! Mind you, when I first saw it, it was buried up to the top of its tracks in mud and my job, with the help of the Territorial Army, was to get it out and repair it.

At the Black Country Living Museum I have made chain, driven the colliery winding engine, operated the anchor forge, run the Newcomen engine and driven cars, motorcycles, trams and trolleybuses - but nothing can quite compare with taking part in the first Fly Run with President.

My knowledge of the canal system still leaves a lot to be desired but somewhere near Milton Keynes I was in the engine room as we ran with a full head of steam on a straight clear length of canal just as the sun came up. It was quite unforgettable.

Almost as memorable was the call from Coseley 'We think the fusible plug has gone!' and many other incidents; from drawing up the original pipework layout in Leviathan, roasting with the Canal Panel on the way to the Bratch, to the innumerable committee meetings; and I haven't been on the boat that much.

Considering that the Black Country Living Museum is not a boat museum, and I do have to remind enthusiasts of that from time to time, we do have a significant collection and probably the most famous canal boat on the system.

President and Kildare are very much part of the public face of the Museum and the Friends of President are one of our greatest assets. The decision to get involved with the boat was, however, not an easy one.

I had known Malcolm Braine since the earliest days of the Museum and when he said he was going to restore President I was able to offer a little help with the original steam plant. It was when the West Midlands County Council was considering taking it on to promote their work with the waterways that we became involved.

The ownership of the boat moved through several stages, as you will read later, until the Black Country Living Museum became the sole owner and Friends of President became the organisation which made it work for us. President is not a Black Country boat, although Kildare is, and it didn't spend much time in the area, but it is an excellent flagship and helps to promote the work of the Museum throughout the country.

As those who have been involved with the boats will know only too well, they are hard mistresses: always wanting more and often awkward. It is a tribute to the many volunteers that the boats are so well cared for and appreciated. It is also remarkable that volunteers often end up spending many, many years with Friends of President.

It would be inappropriate to mention any of the individuals who have made the preservation of President so successful. They know who they are and we would only forget someone; but to all of you may I give my heartfelt thanks. This book is a marvellous tribute to not only the boat but all those who, in whatever way, have ensured that it can celebrate 100 years. The challenge is now to ensure that it can continue in preservation and operation (costs, legislation and eco factors allowing) for many years to come.

Ian N Walden OBE
Museum Director and Chief Executive

Fellows, Morton & Clayton Ltd (1889 - 1948)

Fellows, Morton & Clayton Ltd. was formed in July 1889, taking over the businesses of Fellows, Morton & Co. and William Clayton of Saltley. The first joint Managing Directors were Joshua Fellows, Frederick Morton and Thomas Clayton. It is recorded that they were paid a salary of £600 per annum, and that they were to hold office for seven years. The company quickly became one of the leading carriers and developed their own design of hull, the 'Josher', after Joshua Fellows. The abbreviated form of the company name, F.M.C., seems to have been used from the early days and soon lost the full stops.

Steam powered tugs were first built and trialled in Scotland in 1803 but steam-driven cargo-carrying narrow boats were not developed until the mid 19th century. The Grand Junction Canal Company experimented with a fleet of cargo-carrying narrow boats, but withdrew them following the 'Blow Up Bridge' explosion in 1874, when five tons of gunpowder exploded under Macclesfield Bridge in Regent's Park, London.

FMC inherited ten steam narrow boats of which six were wooden hulled boats (*Speedwell, Phœnix, Hecla, Pirate, Queen & Victoria*), and the other four had mild steel hulls (*Empress, Princess, Duke & Duchess*). They also inherited one wide beam boat, *Wild Rose*, but this was sold in 1892. All these boats had been built in the five years prior to FMC being formed.

The first steamer built by FMC was *Countess* in 1890, at their Fazeley Street dock. The hull of this was also mild steel, and was the last craft that FMC built using that material. The use of mild steel had not proved successful. *Duchess* was sold in 1893, and the other four only lasted a few more years more before being rebuilt.

The building of steamers was transferred to Saltley and the next four boats were rebuilds of the early wooden hulls (*Phœnix, Speedwell, Pirate & Duke*). The second new boat, *Earl*, appeared in 1895 and this also had a wooden hull. All the steamers constructed at Saltley after this date were built with composite hulls, that is, with iron sides and wooden bottoms. The rebuild of *Princess* was the first to appear in this form, followed by a rebuild of *Countess*.

In the years up to 1900, the last of the mild steel hulled boats (*Empress*) was rebuilt and eight new steamers were built at Saltley (*Marquis, Emperor, Prince, Baron, Baroness, Sultan, Count & Colonel*).

Pirate was sold in 1902 and it was not until 1905 that steamers were built again, with *The King* and *Admiral* appearing. *General* and *Monarch* were built in 1907 and 1908 respectively, and *President* and *Viceroy* were built in 1909. *Vulcan*, having first been built as a gas

4

powered boat in 1906, was converted to a steamer in 1910. The last two steamers to be built at Saltley were *Vanguard* and *Victory* in 1911. Also in 1911, *Swan*, a wide beam steamer, was built at Uxbridge and used to work the London end of the Grand Junction Canal. It was never a success and was dismantled two years later.

The End Of The Steamer Era

The period between 1911 and 1915 was the time when FMC had the most narrow boat steamers operating, a total of 27, but the supremacy of the steamer was about to be challenged. The arrival in England of the Bolinder semi-diesel engine in 1911 and its economic advantages brought the heyday of the steamer to a relatively quick end. It was soon appreciated that a diesel engine could provide a roughly equivalent power source set in a much smaller space and without the need for a specialist attendant.

FMC built their first Bolinder powered motor boat, *Linda*, in 1912. They used a steamer hull that they were in the course of building and simply modified the design to accommodate the smaller engine. Experience showed that, without the steam boiler, they were able to load at least another eight tons of cargo - an appreciable increase of revenue-earning capacity. In addition to this, without the need for a driver, the crew could be reduced.

1915 saw the start of the decline in the steamer fleet, with the conversion of *Baron* and *Baroness* to diesel power. During the next three years *Emperor* and *Empress* were converted, *Queen* had all the steam plant removed and became a coke boat, and *Victoria* was sold.

Due to a shortage of Bolinder engines, two more wooden hulled steamers were built at Uxbridge, *Hecla* being rebuilt in 1922, and *Duteous* new in 1923. *Duke* was also dismantled in the same year. The supply of diesel plant then improved and in 1924 eight steamers were converted to motors, *Hecla*, *Princess*, *Countess*, *Sultan*, *Colonel*, *Admiral*, *General* and *Duteous*. A further five were converted in 1925, *Marquis*, *Count*, *The King*, *Monarch* & *President*. Also in that year

Phœnix was dismantled and *Earl* was sold. The remainder of the steamers were converted, *Prince* & *Vanguard* in 1926, *Viceroy*, *Vulcan* and *Victory* in 1927, and finally *Speedwell* in 1928.

Vulcan above lock 11, Buckby. (Photo: Waterways Archive, Gloucester)

Many of the steamers in the FMC fleet had an official photograph, similar to the one showing *Vulcan* above, taken between 1910 and 1912, usually above lock 11 at Buckby on the Grand Junction Canal. Most of these show an impressive wash coming from the propeller, although the lack of a bow wave betrays the fact that the boat is stationary in the water. Close examination of the photographs reveal the rope that is securing the boat to the lock, so that a sharp image could be obtained. The photographic emulsions of those days were much slower.

For many years the only known image of *President* as a steamer was a torn fragment that only just revealed the name of the boat. It was not part of a 'Buckby' photograph but was taken at an unidentified location.

Fifteen 'Buckby' photographs exist today, although it is possible that nine others were taken but have disappeared. The 'missing' images are those of *Admiral*, *Duke*, *Emperor*, *Hecla*, *Monarch*, *Speedwell*, *Viceroy*, *Victoria* and *Victory*.

6

Fellows, Morton & Clayton Ltd went on to become the best known and possibly the most successful of the carrying companies in the country. They operated a fleet of boats that traded over much of the waterway system. The company worked right up until the nationalisation of the waterways in 1948, when its boats were merged with those of the Grand Union Canal Carrying Company.

List of FMC steamers
(hull construction - *wood*, **mild steel**, composite)

Name	Built or entered service	Fate
Admiral	1905	Converted to diesel engine, 1924
Baron	1898	Converted to diesel engine, 1915
Baroness	1898	Converted to diesel engine, 1915
Colonel	1899	Converted to diesel engine, 1924
Count	1899	Converted to diesel engine, 1925
Countess	1890	Rebuilt with composite hull, 1896
Countess	1896	Converted to diesel engine, 1924
Duchess	1888	Sold to H & E Humphrey, 1893
Duke	1888	Rebuilt with wooden hull, 1894
Duke	1894	Dismantled, 1923
Duteous	1923	Converted to diesel engine, 1924
Earl	1895	Sold to Charles Court Jnr, 1925
Emperor	1898	Converted to diesel engine, 1917
Empress	1887	Rebuilt with composite hull, 1897
Empress	1897	Converted to diesel engine, 1919
General	1907	Converted to diesel engine, 1924
Hecla	1885	Rebuilt with wooden hull, 1921
Hecla	1921	Converted to diesel engine, 1924
Marquis	1898	Converted to diesel engine, 1925
Monarch	1908	Converted to diesel engine, 1925
Phœnix	1884	Rebuilt with wooden hull, 1892
Phœnix	1892	Dismantled, 1925
Pirate	1886	Rebuilt with wooden hull, 1893
Pirate	1893	Sold to Thames Conservancy, 1902
President	1909	Converted to diesel engine, 1925

Prince	1898	Converted to diesel engine, 1926
Princess	1887	Rebuilt with composite hull, 1895
Princess	1895	Converted to diesel engine, 1924
Queen	1887	Converted to coke boat, 1916
Speedwell	1884	Rebuilt with wooden hull, 1893
Speedwell	1893	Converted to diesel engine, 1928
Sultan	1899	Converted to diesel engine, 1924
Swan	1911	Dismantled, 1913
The King	1905	Converted to diesel engine, 1925
Vanguard	1911	Converted to diesel engine, 1926
Viceroy	1909	Converted to diesel engine, 1927
Victoria	1887	Dismantled, 1912
Victory	1911	Converted to diesel engine, 1927
Vulcan	1910	Converted to diesel engine, 1927
Wild Rose	1888	Sold, 1892

The Steamer Years
(1909 - 1925)

President was built at a cost of £600, in 1909 by Fellows, Morton & Clayton Ltd at their Saltley dock, which lay between locks 62 and 63 in the Garrison flight on the Birmingham & Warwick Junction Canal, now part of the Grand Union Canal.

Her overall length was 70 feet, the beam was 7 feet 1 inch, and the normal working draught was 3 feet 6 inches when carrying approximately 12 tons. Her deadweight, excluding fuel and water, was 14 tons. The hull was of a composite construction of riveted wrought iron sides with a 3 inch elm bottom. Specifically, this entails the use of nominal ¼ inch rolled iron plates to the sides, bow and stern, all hot riveted by hand. Internal vertical joints are supported by single-row riveted butt straps whilst external joints were iron caulked where required. The stem and stern posts were shaped in forged iron. Rolled iron angles were used for internal footings, gunwale supports, deck supports, and knees within the main bow area.

The main plating was supplied by Robert Heath's famous iron works from either Biddulph or Kidsgrove, in North Staffordshire. It is quite possible that it would have been conveyed to Saltley dock in one of FMC's own boats, maybe one of their steamers, which at that time worked regularly up towards Manchester via the Trent and Mersey Canal.

The hullside to bottom support knees were fashioned with blacksmithed tapered rolled iron, riveted to the hullsides and bolted to the transverse 3 inch thick English elm boards. These boards usually varied in width between 15 and 36 inches. An internal centre line 10 inch wide by 4 inch deep pitch pine keelson was bolted to the elm bottom, requiring only one scarfed end-on joint to provide the 62 foot length. A 6 foot length riveted iron plate foredeck was completed with a T stud, deck hatch, oak deck cross beam and side cants. The gunwales were capped with 2 inch oak, bedded on hot pitch and hair felt, drilled and bolted to the 3 inch gunwale angles. Aft of the fore deck a close fitting riveted collision bulkhead was fitted across the main hull area.

Externally, the hullsides were provided with a complete set of 2½ inch feather edged rubbing guards, riveted into place. The aft counter deck was constructed with heavy cross bearers, overlaid with 2 inch oak compass boards, caulked and heavily pitched prior to hair felting. This was then again overlaid with tight fitting, close nailed, ½ inch oak sheering boards. Beneath the counter a heavy heel plate (the skeg), and its steady bar, the rudder assembly and the heavy duty stern tube were fitted to complete the hull. Internally the plate works were finished with red lead paint and the external hullsides treated with hot pitch and tar. The hull was now ready for the operating plant.

The boiler was a 'Scotch' return tube type boiler made by Ruston Proctor & Co Ltd of Lincoln, costing £65, with a working pressure of 120 psi. Scotch boilers differ dramatically from previous types by using a large number of small diameter tubes, which allow the hot gases to run from the combustion chamber at the rear of the grate, through the water compartment, to an enclosed smoke box at the forward end of the boiler, and eventually to the chimney. This greatly increases the surface heating area. This boiler had 48 tubes and 10 solid stays. It measured 6 feet long and 4 feet diameter. Fuel, usually coke, was kept in bunkers on either side of the boiler and filled from the cabin top. The bunkers together held about 1 ton of coke.

A similar boiler to those installed in the steamers. (Photo: C.P. Weaver)

Water for the boiler was drawn directly from the canal through a filter and mud box as the condensing medium for a jet condenser. The resulting condensate was pumped to a feed tank by a reciprocating air pump in the jet condenser, which was driven by eccentrics from the engine crankshaft. A feed pump, also driven in a similar manner, was used to pump water from the feed tank to the boiler. The excess feed overflowed back into the canal. Normally all running was done with the condenser in circuit, but when occasion demanded the exhaust could be diverted up the funnel.

The engine was a vertical, single crank, tandem compound fully condensing engine built by FMC under licence to a design by W.H. & A.H. Haines Ltd., of Birmingham. Only one photograph of this type of engine is known to have survived, that of *Admiral* (right). The engine is slightly unusual in design, having the flywheel at the forward end of the engine and rotating anticlockwise. The high pressure cylinder size was of 5 inch bore and the low pressure 10 inch, with a stroke of 10 inch. The engine ran at 160 rpm with steam at 110 psi and developed 11 hp.

Haines engine from the steamer Admiral. (Photo: Waterways Archive, Gloucester)

The photograph on the right is of the steamer Earl's propeller, which confirms that the engine rotated in an anti-clockwise direction. (Photo: Waterways Archive, Gloucester)

President's propeller was made of phosphor bronze with a diameter of 34 inches, and a pitch of 38 inches.

With a propeller of this large size and pitch, 200 rpm was considered the maximum for canal use, and 300 rpm for deeper water found in rivers. The 31 inches by 24 inches rudder was unbalanced with the whole bearing area beyond the pivot point. This meant that only half the force produced by the propeller was available for steering the boat.

The roof and sides of the engine and boiler compartments were of riveted iron plate on 2 inch angle iron framings, whilst the boatman's living cabin was built and fitted entirely of timber.

Further works to complete the fit out necessitated the construction of a set of false floors (sectional floor boards or 'shutts') for the hold, and running gear consisting of cross support beams, box mast, running plank stands, full-length top running planks, the cratch assembly, side, top, tippet and deck cloths, hand pump, boathook and a collection of various sized ropes.

It is possible that *President*'s early working life as a steamer would have been spent running the fly service between London, Leicester and Nottingham, with occasional forays on to the London, Braunston and Birmingham route.

The steamers carried a variety of manufactured goods and imported commodities and were seldom used for bulk cargoes such as coal, wheat or gravel. High value goods, such as sugar, tea, soap, tinned goods, paper, chemicals and even HP Sauce also attracted higher tariffs which helped to pay the increased costs of running fly.

Running fly meant travelling non-stop day and night. Steamers were ideal for this type of operation. Whilst it took up to four hours to light the boiler and reach working pressure, once moving it was more economic to run for a long period than to allow the fire to go out and restart the process next morning.

When the steam plant was put into the boat, about 250 cubic feet of cargo space was lost, thus reducing the available revenue earning capacity. Travelling non-stop made up for this to a certain extent. When running on the wide section of the Grand Junction Canal between London and Braunston she would tow a butty, making use of the fact that the locks on this section were wide enough for two boats. Elsewhere, she would normally have worked on her own. She would have kept a strict timetable and the London to Birmingham run would have been completed in 54 hours.

When paired up with a butty, there was a crew of seven, four on *President* (captain, captain's mate, chief driver, assistant driver), and three on the butty. On the steamer, two were working while two rested. The captain would have worked with the assistant driver, and the captain's mate with the driver, so that a senior crew member was always on duty. They worked a shift pattern of approximately three hours, changing at set geographical points rather than by the clock.

The FMC wharf in City Road Basin on the Regent's Canal was the London departure point for the steamers, and they left at 7pm. The change points are listed as Greenford Road Bridge, Uxbridge Lock No.88, Cassiobury Lock No.76, Boxmoor Lock No.63, Cowroast Lock No.46, Slapton Lock No.30, Stoke Hammond Lock No.23, Bradwell Wharf, Stoke Bruerne Top Lock No.14, Buckby Bottom Lock No.13, Braunston, Stockton Bridge No.23, Leamington Bridge No. 40, Hatton Lock No.42, Knowle Top Lock. There is also record of both Hatton top and bottom locks, and Knowle bottom lock as changeover points, instead of the others listed above.

The driver operated all the controls on the engine and fired the boiler, so there had to be some form of communication between the steerer and the driver. The steerer had two lanyards for controls, one to the engine room bell to give engine instructions and the other to the whistle. The bell signals were probably as follows (and are the signals used today):-

one ding - half ahead,
ding pause ding - full ahead,
two dings (no pause) - half astern,
two dings pause two dings - full astern,
three dings (no pause) - stop engine.

'Half' and 'full' would not have been fixed speeds, but an indication of speeding up and slowing down depending on the rapport built up between the steerer and the driver.

The captain of the steamer Duke at Stoke Bruerne in 1896. (Photo: C. Newton)

Steamer captains, whose distinctive uniform included unbleached corduroy trousers, took great pride in the appearance of their boats. Practical blue overalls were worn by the engine driver and his assistant. A curtain protected the engine from dust when firing or cleaning the boiler tubes. There was spartan sleeping accommodation in the cabin, and in front of the boiler a hammock was provided for the driver. Any cooking was done on the 'bottle' stove in the cabin or using the heat from the boiler.

ORDER OF LOCAL GOVERNMENT BOARD,

Form B.—No. 2c

London: KNIGHT & CO., 90 Fleet Street.—18, 1/7-80

REGISTER OF CANAL BOATS.

Birmingham R. Case **Registration Authority.**

1. Registration Number of the boat. ...	1212
2. Name of the boat, or, if there be no name, the number	Prudent
3. Christian Name, Surname, and Address of Owner* ...	Fellows Morton Clayton Ltd Birmingham
4. Christian Name and Surname of Master	James Morfield
5. Route along which the boat is accustomed or intended to ply ...	London & Birmingham
6. Nature of the traffic in which the boat is accustomed or intended to be employed...	General Goods
7. Mode of propulsion; and whether a "wide," or "narrow" boat; and whether to be used as a "fly" boat worked by shifts ...	Steam Narrow
8. Number of cabins in the boat ...	One aft
9. Dimensions and cubical capacity of the cabin or cabins—	

Rule of measurement and of deduction adopted :—§

Byle §
Deduction §

		ft.	in.
After Cabin	Height	5	2
	Length	8	-
	Width	5	10
	Gross cabled capacity	241	1
	Net cabled capacity or free air space	192	11
Fore Cabin	Height		
	Length		
	Width		
	Gross cabled capacity		
	Net cabled capacity or free air space		

10. Date of application for Registration ...	June 8th 1909
11. Date of examination by Officer of Authority	June 8th 1909
12. Date of Registration	June ... 1909
13. Place to which the boat is registered as belonging, for the purposes of the Elementary Education Acts ...	Birmingham
	(_This must be some place which is either a School District, or is part of a School District, and is situate wholly or partly within the Jurisdiction of the Registration Authority: See 40 & 41 Vict., c. 60, s. 7._)
14. Maximum number of persons for which the boat is registered, subject to the conditions prescribed with regard to the separation of the sexes	Four
	[_Note.—In the case of a boat built after the 30th of June, 1878, three children under the age of 12 years may be reckoned, as regards the maximum of free air space, as equivalent to two persons above the age of 12 years. In the case of a boat built prior to the 30th of June, 1878, two children under the age of 12 years may be reckoned as equivalent to one person above the age of 12 years: See Art. 8 a. of the Order_]
15. Observations	FLY BOAT
	4 persons.
	... persons.
	... persons.
	as follows viz:
	Four men, or four women,
16. Initials of Clerk or Chairman of ... Authority acting as the Registration	J. J. R...

*If the boat is owned by a partnership firm, or by a company or association, corporate or unincorporate, state the name of the firm, company, or association, and their principal office or place of business.

† If the boat is a **wide** boat, state the word "wide"; if a **narrow** boat, state the word "narrow."

‡ See Art. 9. New Note to Form 13, and Form 15, § of Instructing Officer's Report] has been adopted in the measurement of the cabin or cabins :—distinguishing, in each case, where necessary, the rule of deduction.

President (fleet No.195) was registered in Birmingham on 23rd June 1909, registration number 1212 (see page 16), as a Fly boat carrying general goods from London to Birmingham, with a crew of either four men or four women.

The Captain was listed as James Woodfield (photograph on the left courtesy of the Woodfield family), who was in charge of the boat until at least 1911.

President's butty featured in correspondence sent to Mr Millner, the General Manager for the southern part of the Grand Junction Canal at Blisworth, on June 15th 1910:-

"Sir the butty boat behind the President engine had three chaps hanging to her in and out of canal bathing they was naked when they passed our house on the boat it was indecent they was going on with it to the station Weedon yours T Dyke"

President was gauged for the Grand Junction Canal (Certificate No. 11682 - see page 18) on 20th February 1911. The Grand Junction Canal Company referred to the steamers as 'engines'. Gauging is the process whereby a boat's capacity is measured by the amount of water it displaces when loaded with a cargo. It became commonplace on major waterways such as the Grand Junction, Oxford and Birmingham canals, as a means of calculating how much cargo was being carried, in order to be able quickly to assess the correct toll.

The boat was taken to a gauging dock and emptied of everything except the working gear necessary for operation. All of the items left on board were listed on the gauging sheet. 'Dunnage' covers the wooden chocks and blocks necessary to secure boxed cargo.

TONS	Dry Inches	Difference	TONS	Dry Inches	Difference	ALTERATIONS Cwt.	DATE
Light	30.44	1.56	21	1.71	1.50		
1	29.21		22	.21			
2	27.65		23	30.56			
3	26.09		24				
4	24.53	1.49	25				
5	23.04		26				
6	21.55		27				
7	20.06		28				
8	18.54	1.20	29				
9	17.34		30				
10	16.17		31				
11	14.94	1.32	32				
12	13.44		33				
13	12.45		34				
14	11.13		35				
15	9.87		36				
16	8.49		37				
17	7.17	1.22	38				
18	5.85		39				
19	4.52		40				
20	3.21		41				

No. 11682

Jellicoe & Co. "President" (Engine)

	Feet	Inches
Length	40	. -
Breadth	7	. 1

	Inches
Draught of Water when Light . . .	19.87
Draught of Water when Laden with 22 Tons	30.43

ARTICLES on Board when WEIGHED.

3 Cross Beams	1 A false Bottom
1 Mast and Case	~~Trusses of Hay~~
1 Pump	~~Bushels of Corn~~
1 Tarpaulings & Side Cloths	~~Cwt of Coals~~ 1 Ton Coke
1 Deck and Cabin Cloth	2 Cwts of Dunnage
3 Gang Planks	
~~Legging Planks~~	One Head and Stern Strap
1 Standards	One Towing Line and Stove

NOTE.—STRIKE OUT ARTICLES NOT ON BOARD.

30th February 1911.

The weights used in the gauging process.These two are situated at the entrance to the Boat Dock at the Black Country Living Museum. (Photo: N. Ratcliffe)

Then a series of one ton weights were carefully lowered into the hull. After four weights had been placed along the bottom boards, the dry side (the distance from the gunwale to the waterline) of the hull was measured in four places (two on each side) and these figures recorded on the working sheet. The sequence was then repeated until the dry side was reduced to a safe minimum. The clerk then averaged the figures so that a value was worked out for the depth for each ton loaded.

The gauging sheet produced from these calculations was copied and distributed to each toll office. From these records, the toll clerk could work out what weight of cargo the boat was carrying. He would measure the dry side of the boat, in the four places and average the results, then look up the figure on the gauging sheet.

The photograph of *Phœnix* being gauged at Buckby shows the toll clerk measuring the dry side using a gauging rod. This instrument contained a graduated floating rule so that the reading could be taken without the clerk having to peer down to water level to note the depth. The image is

19

almost certainly posed. The weight of the crew member standing on the left side of the cabin seems to be tilting the boat so that the reading would have been false (to the advantage of FMC).

Phœnix being gauged at Buckby. (Photo: Waterways Archive, Gloucester)

A certain amount of information concerning the maintenance of *President* has come from the FMC Dock Book. Quite early on it was noted that at the first joint of the hull plates past the aftermost bulkhead in the hold, on the top rubbing strake, the hull measured 7 feet 1½ inches. The comment continued "owing to small bulge on each side - watch wear". It was also noted that this was the first engine to have "lead on SV viz 1/16"." This almost certainly means that there was a 1/16" timing advancement (lead) incorporated in the operation of the slide valve. This would change the timing of the inlet and exhaust of the steam and may have affected the performance of the engine.

Canal Inspector's Journals are another source of information, and four entries can be found regarding *President*, the first on 27th May 1911, when she was inspected at Braunston, the Captain was still James Woodfield, and she was accompanied by the butty *Buckingham*.

Over four years now passes before mention of *President* is found in the surviving toll office books from Brentford. The first of eight entries is 18th June 1915, where it is noted that there was 12.5 inches of freeboard, which according to the gauging record, would suggest that she was carrying about 13 tons. At this time the Captain is listed as Griffiths. On 29th June of the same year she was inspected at Berkhamsted, this time with the butty *James*, and on August 8th, with the butty *Una*, she passed Brentford toll office again carrying 10 ton 12 cwt (hundredweight).

President at Buckby, c1911. This is not the official 'Buckby' image, but another photograph taken shortly afterwards. This photograph was not found until the late 1990's.

In November 1918, the boiler was damaged by Charlie Court (who had a reputation for wrecking boilers, he ruined at least three). The boiler was taken out and sent to J. Wild of Oldham for repair. To keep the boat working, it was replaced by a repaired boiler which had originally come from *Vulcan*.

A copy of a telegram has survived from Mr (Mac) Anderson (FMC Southern Area Manager) to Mr Millner, sent on 31st October 1920, saying "Steamers President King and butties passed Cowley noon Friday Cargoes most urgent please arrange pass Buckby Braunston to clear Warwick stoppages"

The boat was repainted in 1921, as noted from an entry in a Canal Inspection Journal. It appears that FMC boats were regularly serviced and repainted in an approximate four year cycle although there is evidence that on many occasions the boats were docked as a result of an infringement notice issued by the Sanitary Inspector.

When these notices were issued, two copies would have been sent to FMC. Once they had rectified the fault (repaired the leak, repainted the cabin, issued a new water can or any of the myriad faults that could be found by a zealous inspector), they were required to return the second copy duly certifying that all was now in order.

On May 4th 1922, she again passed Brentford toll office, this time with the butty *Twyford* carrying 14 ton 11 cwt. She passed on May 16th, carrying an incredible 18 ton 11 cwt of Lyles sugar and hemp but there is no mention of a butty this time.

On 25th October and again on 21st December 192*, *President* was inspected at Braunston, without a butty. By now the Captain was listed as F.Woodward, and on both occasions there were only three men on board, which suggests that they were no longer running fly. The last record for 1922 was again passing Brentford carrying 13 ton 12 cwt.

Finally, in 1923 there were three more entries for Brentford, August 2nd carrying 13 ton 4 cwt, December 19th (14 ton 16 cwt) and December 28th (14 ton 18 cwt). This was the last official recording of *President* as a steamer, although it was nearly eighteen months before she was taken to the FMC yard at Saltley to be fitted with a semi-diesel engine.

The Diesel Years
(1925 - 1974)

In May 1925, it was *President*'s turn to have the steam engine and boiler removed, and in its place a 15hp single cylinder Bolinder NE engine was fitted. This engine was supplied by Pollock's of Faversham at a cost of £235. The total cost of the conversion was £287.

The relatively simple operation of these semi-diesel direct reversing engines made them particularly suitable for use on the canals. The Bolinder's Crude Oil engine is of the two cycle type, delivering a power impulse for each revolution of the flywheel. It has no valves, cams, gears or electric sparking device and the construction is such that all the parts work automatically and cannot be thrown out of adjustment.

With her carrying capacity increased by in excess of eight tons and the crew reduced by two, *President*, now no longer a fly boat and bearing the newly introduced colour scheme of red, yellow and green, gets her first mention as a motor in a letter, dated July 13th 1925, from FMC to Mr Millner at Blisworth saying that "We have loaded our motor boat President and Beatrice at Shipley to-day for Stoke Bruerne and the boats will be leaving the Colliery to-night." Shipley Colliery is on the Erewash Canal and, with her butty, they could have loaded 50 tons of coal for Stoke Bruerne.

In August 1926, on the 10th and 25th, she is listed in the Brentford toll records as passing through with her butty, *Beatrice*, carrying 24 ton 12 cwt and 28 ton 11 cwt respectively. Then on 21st October, she was gauged by the Grand Junction Canal Company - Certificate No 12148 (see page 25). Comparing this certificate with the previous one as a steamer shows slight variations in the articles she was weighed with, and the table now goes up to 30 tons, as opposed to 22 tons as a steamer.

In 1927 there are nine entries, between July and December, for the toll office at Brentford where the weights carried were anything from 20 to nearly 23 tons. The weights noted for *Beatrice* were from 23 to nearly 27 tons.

There were also two inspections carried out in 1927, the first on 27th August at Nottingham, where the captain was listed as T. Simpson, and the second was at Ilkeston on September 23rd, where the captain had now changed to Thomas Webb.

Thomas Webb shown sitting on the butty Beatrice. He continued to command President up until 1937. (Photo: Unknown)

His crew for most of the time were his wife Mary and his daughter Hannah, seen steering in the photograph left. (Photo: D. McDougall)

No. 1248

Fellows Morton & Clayton Ld   M/B "President".

	Feet	Inches
Length	70	-
Breadth	7	1¼

	Inches
Draught of Water when Light . . .	16.80
Draught of Water when Laden with 30 Tons	50.12

Stowage 45' 12"

ARTICLES on Board when WEIGHED.

4 Cross Beams	A false Bottom
Mast and Case	~~Trusses of Hay~~
Pump	~~Bushels of Corn~~
Tarpaulings & Side Cloths	½Cwt. of Coals
Deck and Cabin Cloth	1 Cwt. of Dunnage
4 Gang Planks	One Head and Stern Strap
Legging Planks	One Towing Line and Stove
3 Standards	Motor Engine complete
1 Shore Plank	110 Gallons Oil
1 Log	

NOTE.—STRIKE OUT ARTICLES NOT ON BOARD

Dspt October 1926.

Lett 1689   IN - 12.40

Fellows Morton & Clayton Ld   M/B 'President'

TONS	Dry Inches	Difference	TONS	Dry Inches	Difference	ALTERATIONS		
							Cwts.	DATE
Light.	33.70	1¼	21	10.28	1.10	Ded	5	17/1/14
1	32.56		22	9.18		Add	"	4.6.35
2	31.42		23	8.09				
3	30.29	1¼	24	6.49	1.10			
4	9¼		25	5.80				
5	28.00		26	4.78				
6	26.86		27	3.68				
7	25.72	1.42	28	2.59	1.10			
8	24.59		29	1.49				
9	23.16		30	.39				
10	22.34		31	33.32 / 16.80				
11	24.22		32	50.12				
12	20.10		33					
13	19.01	1.09	34					
14	17.92		35					
15	16.73		36					
16	15.74		37					
17	14.65	1.09	38					
18	13.56		39					
19	12.47		40					
20	11.39		41					

Throughout 1928 there are regular mentions in the Brentford toll office records of *President* passing (17 in total), with similar tonnages being carried as listed for the previous year. The same applies to her butty *Beatrice*. One entry, for 13th August, has *President*'s cargo listed as Lyles sugar, and *Beatrice*'s as milk and spelter, a zinc alloy.

Only one inspection has been found for this year, and that was at Nottingham on 10th November. The same applies to 1929 with the one inspection, again at Nottingham, here it was noted that the boat had been painted in July of that year.

These inspections were the result of the Canal Boat Acts of 1877 and 1884 which laid down that every boat with an accommodation cabin had to be registered and regularly inspected. The registrations and inspections were carried out by urban and rural sanitary authorities, which kept records of the registrations and inspections in journals. Health Registration Journals hold a lot of information about a boat, including its name and number, the name and address of its owner, its dimensions and construction, including what cabin space it has, as well as the name of its master at the time of registration. Inspection journals also show who was on board at the time of inspection and the condition of the boats, including the last time it was painted.

Three inspections have been found for 1931, one at Leicester on 19th January, and two at Nottingham, the first on November 8th, where it was noted that the boat was last painted in the previous March, and the second on December 18th. This latter inspection is the only mention of a butty other than *Beatrice* for the whole of the period between 1925 and 1937; on this occasion it is listed as *Yiewsley*.

On March 15th 1932, *President* was examined in Birmingham for re-registration as a motor boat. The long delay between conversion and re-registration was possibly due to the fact that she had not worked to Birmingham in the intervening years. She was registered in Birmingham on 15th April - Registration No. 1541 (see page 27). The number of people that the boat was registered for was three men or three women or man, wife and one child (if male under 14, or female under 12) or if fly

ORDER of LOCAL GOVERNMENT BOA

Form B.—No. 2c.

Register of Canal Boats

Birmingham REGISTRATION AUTHORITY.

1. Registration Number of the Boat ...   1547·1

2. Name, or, if there be no name, the number of canal boat examined ...   Provident

3. Christian Name, Surname, and Address of Owner*   Fellows Morton & Clayton Co. Birmingham

4. Christian Name and Surname of Master ...   Thomas Webb

5. Route along which the boat is accustomed or intended to ply ...   Birmingham to London

6. Nature of the traffic in which the boat is accustomed or intended to be employed ...   General Goods

7. Mode of propulsion; and whether a "wide" or "narrow" boat; and whether to be used as a "fly" boat worked by shifts ...   Motor Narrow (Fly)

8. Number of cabins in the boat ...   One Aft

9. Dimensions and cubical capacity of the cabin or cabins :—

Rule of measurement and of deduction adopted :—
Rule B
Deduction 15%

		ft.	in.
After Cabin	Height	5	4
	Length	8	1
	Width	5	7
	Gross cubical capacity	240	8
	Net cubical capacity or free air space	192	7
Fore Cabin	Height		
	Length		
	Width		
	Gross cubical capacity		
	Net cubical capacity or free air space		

10. Date of applic... n for Registration ...   March 12 1932.

11. Date of examination by Officer of Authority   March 15th 1932.

12. Date of Registration ...   15th April 1932.

13. Place to which the boat is registered as belonging, for the purposes of the Elementary Education Acts   Birmingham

(This must be some place which is either a School District, or is part of a School District, and is situate wholly or partly within the Jurisdiction of the Registration Authority. See 40 & 41 Vict. c. 60, s. 7.)

14. Maximum number of persons for which the boat is registered, subject to the conditions prescribed with regard to the separation of the sexes   Three.

Note.—In the case of a boat built after the 30th of June, 1878, there children under the age of 12 years may be reckoned, for regards the minimum of free air space, as equivalent to two persons above the age of 12 years. In the case of a boat built prior to the 30th of June, 1878, two children under the age of 12 years may be reckoned as equivalent to one person above the age of 12 years. See Art. 8 a of the Order.)

As a "Fly" boat worked by shifts— { ...   persons

Otherwise than as a "Fly" boat— { In After Cabin ...   3   persons { In Fore Cabin ...   persons

15. Observations ...   As follows viz:—
Three Men or Three Women

or

Three Men or Three Women

or

Two Men & a Boy. Boat worked by shifts.

A Man over this age are one third. The older if male to be under fourteen and if female under twelve years of age.

Your Obern,
Your Obern,

16. Initials of Clerk or Chairman of the Council acting as the Registration { ...   W. Gilbin Town Clerk

63

27

working then four men working shifts. It is very unlikely that she ever worked fly as a motor. The master at the time of registration was still Thomas Webb.

In 1933, journeys were started between London and Birmingham along the improved and widened Grand Union Canal and her main cargo was coal. In June, July and October 1934 she was inspected at Birmingham and it was noted that she had been painted earlier in the year during February. From a later inspection it would also appear that she was painted again in November. On November 21st she was gauged for the Birmingham Canal Navigations - Registration No 1832.

Carriage tickets which have survived show that in January and March 1935 there were two trips each to Alperton and Willesden with *Beatrice*, carrying approximately 50 tons of coal between them on each trip. Two more inspections occurred at Birmingham in February and March, and one at Brentford in July, and another at Nottingham in October.

Five more inspections are listed at Birmingham during 1936, and then, according to the FMC Dock Book, she was docked at Saltley for an overhaul in January 1937. April of that year saw two further trips to Alperton with nearly 50 tons of coal. At an inspection at Birmingham on 13th May, Thomas Webb is listed as the captain and *Beatrice* the accompanying butty for the last time. The next two, in January (Leicester) and July (Nottingham) 1938 have Thomas Boswell as captain and the butty is *Penkridge*. In February 1940 she was docked at Uxbridge for another overhaul according to the dock book, and on 31st May she was inspected at Nottingham, this time with the butty *Natal*.

Between January and August 1941 *President* was inspected five times at Birmingham with the butty *Keswick*. During the final one of these, the captain, who was still Thomas Boswell, was issued with a caution for "Top and sides of cabin leaking". The last recorded inspection for 1941 at Nottingham shows that the captain, S. Higgins, was booked for overcrowding under Section 8a of the Canal Boat Regulations 1878 for having 2 adults and 4 children in the cabin.

In 1942 the boat was inspected ten times at Birmingham and once at Nottingham, where a caution was issued for overcrowding again, the captain had now changed to R. Aston. At one of these inspections in May, cautions were issued for the certificate to be renewed, and the boat was "dirty and requiring repainting".

More inspections followed in 1943, but the butty had now changed to *Roach*. She also received another overhaul at Saltley in April. In 1944, some journeys with different loads took *President* to Ellesmere Port, Liverpool and Manchester, and Wolverhampton inspections started showing up in the records with *Keswick* back as the usual butty. During 1943 and 1944 the captain is listed as R. Aston, Albert Aston and A. Ashton; these could all refer to the same person. One caution issued referred to the "registration certificate in pieces" and "boat leaks causing flooding".

By December 4th 1944, the captain had changed to W. Evans, and *President* was known to have travelled from Ellesmere Port to Bloxwich with *Keswick* carrying 44.3 tons of wheat. Inspections continued to be recorded at Birmingham and Wolverhampton during 1945 with the same captain. In November of that year, as a single motor, she carried 17.5 tons of tubes from Autherley to Ellesmere Port with a return load of 20 tons of spelter to Birmingham.

FMC finally parted company with *President* in May 1946, when she was sold to Ernest Thomas Ltd., a Walsall based coal carrier. A year later, in 1947, ownership passed to George & Matthews (1924) Ltd., of Wednesbury, and in March and April 1947 there are four load permits which have survived (two from each month) showing that *President* carried 20 tons of coal per trip from Otherton to Stourport along the Staffs & Worcs Canal. The steerer's name was Clegg.

She was re-gauged for the BCN on September 1st 1948 - No 1832 (see page 30). This certificate shows the succession of owners, FMC, Ernie Thomas (successively crossed out) and George & Matthews (1924) Ltd.

George matthews (924) L^d

Late Register N...........

Sept 1st 1948

E Showers,

Date when Gauged, Weighed, and Measured. 21-11-34

Tipton Station.

B.C.N. Register. No. *1552*

Owner .... Address .... W Lampton

Calindon Meter Boat. Name *President* No. .....

Extreme Length 76·42 Extreme Width 7·41

Stowage 45·4 Stowage ..30 6·11

Draught when Light 1·65 / 4·32 Draught when laden with 24 Tons 50·26

Articles on Board when Weighed ....
.... 30 ....

Tons	Dry Inches	Difference	Tons	Dry Inches	Difference	Tons	Dry Inches	Difference	Tons	Dry Inches	Difference	ALTERATIONS	
												Cwts.	DATE
	36·27	1·35		10·50									
Light	34·92	·44	21	9·37		42							
1	34·92		22	8·24		43							
	33·57		23	7·11	1·13	44							
2	32·22		24	6·..	·09	45							
3	30·87	1·28	25	5·98		46							
4	29·59	·83	26	4·85		47							
5	28·31		27	3·72		48							
6	27·03		28	2·59	1·13	49							
7	25·76	1·19	29	1·46		50							
8	24·56		30	·33		51							
9	23·37		31			52							
10	22·18		32			53							
11	20·99	1·18	33			54							
12	19·81		34			55	35·94						
13	18·63		35				32·41						
14	17·45		36				33						
15	16·27		37				36·27						
16	15·11	1·16	38										
17	13·75		39										
18	12·79		40										
19	11·63	1·13	41										
20	10·42												

In the early 1950s, British Waterways North West Division were actively acquiring boats for their maintenance fleet. In 1953, George & Matthews took the opportunity to sell *President*. She had come to the end of her commercial carrying life and became a maintenance craft working on the Trent and Mersey, Macclesfield and Shropshire Union Canals.

In 1953 *President* was noted as being extensively reconditioned at Gorton Yard, which was on the Stockport Branch of the Ashton Canal. The photograph shown on the right is believed to be of *President*.

(Photo: Jim Peden)

The photograph on the left was published in the 'Gorton & Openshaw Reporter (including the Droylsden and Clayton Herald)', issued on September 18th 1953, with an article entitled 'Ruin hides a dry-dock at Openshaw'. The article included the information that "...Moored outside the dry dock this week is the 70ft motor barge "President" now undergoing the final stages of a complete overhaul. Forty years old, the vessel is powered by a single-cylinder diesel engine of a type seldom seen nowadays. Developing 18hp., the engine is primed by a device resembling a huge blow-lamp which raises the cylinder temperature to the required ignition point for starting. The boat, formerly a trading vessel, was built in the Midlands and now operates from Marple on maintenance work."

It was reported in the Docks & Inland Waterways magazine 'Waterways' Vol 6 No. 53, that on the 24th January 1961 she pulled a sunken butty out of Harecastle Tunnel.

In the mid 1960's, whilst in the ownership of the British Waterways Board (which had taken over from the Docks and Inland Waterways Executive in 1962), the Bolinder engine was removed and replaced with a two cylinder Armstrong Siddeley engine.

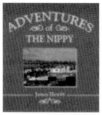 From the book 'Adventures of the Nippy' by James Hewitt there is the following from October 1967:-

"We went out to the wharf where an old josher motor boat lay, thoroughbred of the canals, basking in the early morning sun. She was loaded with 300 steel piles. "Deliver that lot to the piling gang at Disley and fetch her back," he said, handing me the keys. I glanced at the name on her cabin side. It was 'President'."

"I unlocked the doors and then started her engine, an air-cooled two cylinder Armstrong Siddeley, and whilst it warmed up I lit the stove, which turned out to be a primitive affair shaped like a bottle."

""Clean your boat out tomorrow," he advised. He was right about the need to clean her out since she was indeed rather grubby, and the next day I stripped everything moveable out of the cabin and engine room before setting about cleaning it. Working forward, I dug the clay and chippings, remains of earlier loads, out of the hold to prepare for the next consignment of piles, before finally washing her down."

"Marple Section was subdivided into two lengths, Marple and Macclesfield with 'President' shared between. She was now required in the Macclesfield area which had their own crew so they took over."

(He continues the story a few pages later)
"....... A thaw set in about this time along with sorry news of 'President'. She had been taken to the annual Bosley stoppage and the Macclesfield crew had left her overnight in the filled chamber of number two. The lock keeper, who should have known better, assured them that she would be safe since the bottom gates did not leak, but he was mistaken. On the following morning the lock was found to be partly emptied causing 'President's rudder and skeg to be damaged on the sill. They took her to Northwich where she was laid up until noticed by an enthusiast of steam."

President ended her time as a diesel powered boat on the River Weaver at Northwich. Her engine was salvaged and the hull abandoned and left to sink. The remains were offered for sale in 1973.

First Restoration
(1974 - 1982)

The idea of restoring a Fellows Morton & Clayton steam narrow boat had occupied the thoughts of a few canal enthusiasts over the years, since the remarkable upsurge in interest in a mode of transport which, due to its very nature, was in danger of passing from the scene unnoticed. The part played by the Inland Waterways Association and such books as Tom Rolt's classic 'Narrow Boat' undoubtedly ensured that a way of life enjoyed by a race of hard working people traversing the 'silent highways' was recorded for posterity.

During the early 1950s, Malcolm Braine was working at Ernest Thomas's Old Birchills Dock at Walsall. Saddened by the sight of ex-FMC steamers being cut up for their scrap value, he made a conscious, but at that time impossible, decision - to have a hand in restoring one of these magnificent vessels, maybe even transforming it back to steam power.

Time passed and various opportunities to own one of these old steamers came and went. In about 1960 there was a chance of buying *Monarch* for £350. He turned down the option, because he was still looking for premises and didn't have the necessary funds available for a full steamer project. In 1963 he did buy *Countess*, by this time renamed *Victory*, but sold her again in 1965.

In 1972, Malcolm had built and fitted out a 60 foot pleasure boat for his friend Nicholas Bostock, and had mentioned to him his idea for an FMC steamer restoration project. Nicholas had shown great interest. Then twelve months later, in 1973, whilst looking at one of the British Waterways Board's regular tender lists, he spotted *President* listed amongst many other craft lying derelict on the River Weaver at their Hayhurst and Town Yards. His immediate thoughts were "it's now or never".

President (on left) at Hayhurst Yard. (Photo: M. Braine)

The hull was in a sad state, half submerged and stripped by vandals of anything of value; the woodwork of the cabin was rotting away; the platework was corroded and rusted where it was exposed to the ravages of the polluted and highly saline river water; yet the once proud name *President* could just be discerned on the cabin sides.

This sight, and the thought of one day recreating the great age of steam on the canals, were the deciding factors which led to a partnership being formed between Malcolm Braine and Nicholas Bostock, the prime objective being to buy and restore the boat to its former glory. They

34

agreed to share the costs equally although, at the time, they hadn't made any plans on how to proceed.

President was successfully purchased for the sum of £1513.60p including 10% VAT, along with four other narrow boats.

The Anderton Boat Lift was closed at this time for emergency repairs so they were unable to organise the immediate removal of *President* and the other boats that were purchased. However, British Waterways Board finally agreed to temporarily open the lift to allow the

The convoy at Audlem. (Photo: M. Braine)

boats off the Weaver. The boats were towed behind the BCN tug Birchills onto the Trent & Mersey Canal, southwards to Middlewich, across to and down the Shropshire Union Canal, up the Wolverhampton 21 and finally to Norton Canes Dock by way of the Wyrley & Essington Canal.

A resting place was found for *President* where she was sunk to preserve the hull. She lay there for two and a half years awaiting her turn for restoration, before being re-floated on the 20th July 1976. She was winched out onto the dock on the 27th July and was carefully inspected.

A provisional plan was then agreed for a work programme that would restore and maintain the boat for the next five years. The budget was set at £15,000 to undertake the complete project, including the steam plant.

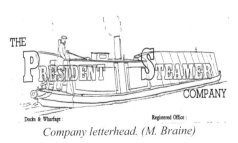
Company letterhead. (M. Braine)

An agreement to form a partnership between Nicholas and Malcolm resulted in the 'President Steamer Company' being registered on the 22nd March 1977 and formalised on the 10th May of the same year.

All labour and materials were to be supplied, at cost, by Malcolm's company, and he would organise and oversee the five year period of restoration and maintenance. Nicholas took on the role as organiser for publicity, crew recruitment and the work entailed in the setting up of the sailing schedules.

Views of both sides. (Photos: N. Bostock)

Seventy years of hard work had taken its toll, which was plain to see when she was winched up onto the dock. The task of restoration began with the renewal of the bottom in three inch thick elm and the fitting of a new oak keelson, stretching from the fore end, back to the boiler room bulkhead. The boards towards the stern remained in sound order with a projected further wear life of about ten years.

Once in the workshop the hullside plating required considerable straightening, finally allowing the fitment of new two inch oak gunwales. Some areas of platework had suffered degradation during years of contact with the heavily salt-laden River Weaver. Others were thin due to wear and tear or corrosion that had built up during years of little or no maintenance.

It was decided that, where necessary, underwater areas of plating would have to be overplated, while those areas

View towards the stern. (Photo: N. Bostock)

above the waterline would be gusset plated, that is, defective areas cut out and replaced with new welded plate. Although Malcolm would have preferred to have hot-riveted the restoration throughout, welding was a less expensive option and within budget. They were also faced with the difficult task of removing the poured concrete sealing ballast which had been laid within the counter area. Progress with the project was sometimes spasmodic, dependant on the availability of the workforce.

Malcolm was fortunate to have been given FMC's details for the boiler/engine room and aft cabin superstructure which helped him to achieve an accurate rebuild. The former was constructed with riveted steel and the boatman's cabin was built and fitted out in timber in the true traditional style.

Prior to launching, other works included the engine and boiler beds, and the external stern gear. The internal platework was cleaned down and thoroughly painted and the external coachpainting was carried out.

With the boat having been wheeled out of the workshops it was set up on the waterside launching skids and the external hullsides were given a good thick coating of hot pitch and tar. Then on the 18th June 1977, without ceremony, *President* slid back into the deep pristine waters of the Cannock Extension Canal. She was now ready for the next stages towards her completion and the re-birth of FMC in steam.

Since *President*'s purchase in October 1973, Malcolm and Nicholas had explored various avenues that might lead to a suitable marine steam engine and boiler, plus all the other necessary gear to complete the installation. This task was made difficult by the knowledge that, as far as it was known, all the original engines and boilers from the FMC steamer fleet had been scrapped after their removal.

By chance early in 1974 Malcolm came across a horizontal 38 x 54 inch marine boiler, with 64 two inch tubes, in a scrapyard at Gobowen in Shropshire. They bought it without further research for £100 and transported it back to Norton Canes.

The Plenty boiler. (Photo: M. Braine)

They had made various contacts with active members of the marine steam world. The first was George Watkins, who was contacted at Bristol University following advice from Richard Hutchings, who was the Curator at Stoke Bruerne Museum. George's response to Malcolm's first letter, sent on the 4th August 1976, was to turn up at the yard the following Saturday morning with his auto-cycle. Malcolm described this as "a privilege to meet this extremely kind, truly delightful and unassuming man".

Malcolm's intention was to first show him the boat, but on passing the Gobowen boiler he became quite ecstatic, running towards it and crying "it's a Plenty, I'm sure it is ,where on earth did you find it?" This meant nothing to Malcolm but he was quickly informed that they had bought a boiler made by Plenty & Son Ltd (Newbury) in about 1864. Clearly, it was a real museum piece but enthusiasm was soon dampened when, after inspection, George pronounced the boiler to be in need of major repairs and worse, it was too small for their purpose.

For the record it was eventually sold to the Dorothea Restoration Co., for the original purchase price. They restored it to working order for use in a Windermere launch.

George's enthusiasm, visits, and freely given advice over the next 12 months, (accompanied by numerous installation sketches sent by post), were invaluable. It was some time later that Nicholas sent Malcolm a reprint of an extract taken from 'The Steamboat Association of Great Britain' Newsletter of September 1975, listing many of George's accomplishments. This explained why he was held in such high esteem within the world of steam; much of this was not known to Malcolm despite many hours of discussion. Such was the modesty of the man.

Nicholas too had made a valuable contact with another well known man of steam, Philip Weaver, author of 'Steam on Canals'. Again he gave so freely of his time, knowledge and expertise that Nicholas and Malcolm would always remain very grateful to him.

In the Autumn of 1976 the Kennet & Avon Trust announced that, due to operating difficulties on an isolated section of the canal between Burbage and Pewsey in Wiltshire, they were disposing of the *Leviathan* at a cost of £2250, a former Birmingham Canal 'Joey' or day boat which had been fitted

On the K & A. (Photo: Unknown)

out between 1972 and 1975 for passenger carrying, and was powered by steam. An inspection of this vessel revealed that the boiler was a horizontal, coal-fired Scotch return tube marine unit, of a similar size and type to those installed in some of the FMC steamers.

The five foot diameter, five foot long riveted steel boiler was made in 1928 by Muir & Findlay at their Parkhead works, Glasgow. There were 60 two inch diameter fire tubes with a heating surface of some 140 square feet. Working pressure was 100psi. It also had the major benefit of having been recently re-tubed at the old G.W.R. Swindon Works and carried a current safety certification for use in a passenger boat.

Propulsion had been by use of a barring engine, transmitting its power to a Hotchkiss Cone propulsion unit, mounted through the bottom of the boat. Both of these were unsuitable for their needs but other items like the feed water pumps proved to be of great value.

Removing the boiler from Leviathan. (Photo: M. Braine)

On the 12th November 1976, a lorry was hired to go to Wootton Rivers to retrieve the boiler and steam plant which was lifted out by a local crane hire firm. They arrived on site at 8am and their first task was to loose off and lift away the superstructure covering the boiler and machinery space. Next they freed off the boiler in order that it could be craned on to the lorry. Finally, the engine, pumps and other ancillary gear were removed and stowed safely with the boiler.

With the superstructure replaced, the crane was dispatched back to its Swindon base. The site was cleared by 12 noon and their journey back to Norton Canes was described as hair-raising. Before even leaving the site they were aware that their four ton lorry had in excess of six tons aboard.

The overloaded lorry. (Photo: M. Braine)

Their arrival at Norton Canes at 5pm was accompanied by huge sighs of relief all round and Malcolm was grateful, as ever, for the hard working support of willing volunteers.

Throughout the whole of the operation they were greatly helped by Ken Taylor, the lock keeper at Wootton Rivers, who also kindly agreed to look after *Leviathan*'s remains until her sale in January 1977 to Mr. T. G. Round for £900.

The possibility of finding a steam engine identical to the original had been fully explored over many years, and had proved fruitless. The choice lay between having a full size replica built or continuing the search for a period engine of similar power output.

The hunt for what they believed to be a suitable engine ended with the purchase of a Rowhedge two cylinder marine unit, with a 4½ inch bore and a 6 inch stroke. It had been listed amongst 65 lots of steam plant, to be sold by L.V. Nelson & Co Ltd., who were based at Catherine de Barnes Wharf, Solihull. It was priced at £1350 to be seen running. Nicholas and Malcolm visited Mr. Nelson and were able to view the engine working, albeit not under load. The engine was reputed to have been stripped, rebuilt and in sound working condition, Mr. Nelson having written extensively on the works he had carried out. They settled on a purchase price of £1250 and the engine was taken to Norton Canes. Mr. Nelson's extensive treatise, which they hoped would make both valuable and interesting reading, proved later to be interesting but certainly not valuable.

The Rowhedge engine. (Photo: N. Bostock)

However, when tested under load in *President* it became apparent that a major overhaul would be necessary in order to meet the minimum standards set by the new operating routine. The engine was removed and completely dismantled for inspection. Resulting from this, all the crankshaft journals were built up by metal deposition (spraying) and reground to a uniform size. Likewise, all the bearings were re-metalled and bored to suit, special attention being paid to the line boring of the main bearings. Excessive wear and clearance in both sets of valve gear were removed by fabrication of new ends to all of the links and fitting new bushes and hardened pins. Improved lubrication was catered for by fitting a larger displacement lubricator in the steam line and large capacity drip-feed lubricators to the three main bearings. The engine was directly coupled, by means of a 2¼ inch diameter tubular stainless steel shaft equipped with 'Layrub' joints, to a right handed, three-bladed, 31 inch diameter, 43 inch pitch bronze propeller specially manufactured by Bruntons of Sudbury to suit this particular installation.

Other non-standard equipment fitted to *President* included a Penberthy 'Instant-Start' injector to supplement the boiler feed pumps described above, a bilge ejector and a heat exchanger to provide the pre-heat of the feed water by the exhaust steam, with provision for bypassing the exchanger and directing steam over the side for tunnel work. Normally, the exhaust was directed up the funnel after leaving the heat exchanger. The impressive two-tone brass whistle was formerly fitted to the *Gaiety*, a well-known pleasure steamer which operated downstream from Evesham on the Warwickshire Avon. The displacement lubricator and several other items of steam equipment also came from this source.

The large diameter funnel, made to the exact measurements of the original, folded down when negotiating low bridges and tunnels, and for the same reason, the safety valve steam pipe had been made easily detachable.

The boiler in place, coal chutes top left and right. (Photo: N. Bostock)

43

Following the installation of the engine and boiler, the boatman's cabin was fitted out in the traditional manner, which included an original Eagle Boat Stove (known as a bottle stove) and a period brass oil lamp. The famous roses and castles of narrow boat decoration were not overdone by FMC, and only appear on the fold down table in the cabin and on the inside faces of the stern doors. The panels were then painted on either side of the cabin giving the carrier's and the boat's name together with the registration and fleet numbers, and also the number 1396 under the carrier's name. This is the Waterman's Hall or River Thames equivalent of a gauging number. The rather austere black, white and blue colour scheme of the steamers, was later changed by FMC when the motors took over, and became the more familiar red, green and yellow.

Finally, *President* was re-rigged exactly as she had been in her carrying days, with new false floors in the hold, cratch, mast, stand, uprights, running planks and a full set of cloths suitably lettered with the Company's name and fleet number. Even a canvas curtain was made as in the original boat to hang between the boiler and the engine to prevent dust falling on the machinery whilst the boiler tubes were being cleaned.

The test run. (Photo: N. Bostock)

The main work of restoration was completed early in 1978 and a test run was made on April 11th of that year along the Cannock Extension

Canal from Norton Canes to Pelsall Junction and back. Work resulting from the test run together with the finishing details was completed by August 1978 and *President* was at last ready for her maiden voyage. This, with her standard crew of four and five tons of best Welsh steam coal aboard, was to the Inland Waterways Association National Rally of Boats at Titford Pools on the BCN. She went there via the Wyrley & Essington Canal, to Horseley Fields Junction, and on to the Old Birmingham Main Line over the Bank Holiday in August 1978.

Her owners were proud to be presented with the Alfred Ritchie Challenge Cockerel for the best turned out working boat. After the rally the boat was taken to Malcolm Braine's base at Great Haywood on the Trent &

Displaying the trophy. (Photo: N. Bostock)

Mersey Canal by way of the BCN to Aldersley Junction and along the Staffs & Worcs Canal. By October of the same year she was back at Norton Canes Dock.

Ellesmere Port. (Photo: N. Bostock)

In July 1979, *President* visited the Black Country Museum, followed by a trip to Ellesmere Port, with display days at Fazeley Street Wharf Birmingham, Wolverhampton, Norbury Junction, Market Drayton, Audlem, Nantwich and Chester on the way. From here she travelled to the National Rally at Northwich via the Manchester Ship Canal and Weston Marsh Lock. In October she travelled south again to Stourbridge and back to Norton Canes via the Black Country Museum and Birmingham.

It had been hoped to keep *President* in commission with the help of sponsorship, advertising, film work, and the occasional carrying of sample cargoes, and to be exhibited from time to time at museums on the canal system.

However, the cost of running and maintaining the boat proved to be too high and in June 1980, the following advert appeared in Funnel No. 23, the journal of the Steam Boat Association.

FOR SALE:
Share in steam narrow boat PRESIDENT, ex Fellows, Morton & Clayton Ltd., Immaculately restored to 1909 original and fully described in FUNNEL No 20, Up to 50% shareholding available either singly or with grouped interests. Vessel fully certified in all respects and in first class condition.

There were no takers.

On the way to Walthamstow. (Photo: Unknown)

1980 saw the boat heading off for Stoke Bruerne in May via Horseley Fields and Warwick Bar. Later, in August, complete with the restored FMC butty *Northwich*, she continued down the Grand Union Canal and on to the IWA National Waterways Festival at Walthamstow on the Lee Navigation. In September the boats returned to Stoke Bruerne and stayed there as Blisworth Tunnel was closed for repairs and did not reopen for four years.

The National Rally & Waterside Arts Festival in 1981 was held in Godalming on the River Wey. *President* attended this rally after visiting a Steam Spectacular at Soulbury in July, and then returned to Stoke Bruerne again. The following year, 1982, to get around the tunnel closure, she again went south on the Grand Union to Brentford, up the Thames to Oxford and ended up at the Black Country Museum.

On 25th October 1982, *President* was listed for sale as Lot 54 at Christie's Auction House in London, with a reserve of £20,000.

The full entry from the catalogue was as follows:-

"Lot 54 - The steam driven canal narrowboat 'President' originally built June 1909 and operated by Fellows Morton & Clayton Ltd., Fleet No. 195, Measurements overall: Length approx 70ft 9in., Beam 7ft 0in., Draft 3ft 2in. The wrought iron, steel and wood hull rebuilt 1976 with elm bottom boards, pitch pine and oak keelson, wrought iron knees, cast iron stern bar and riveted rudder, to as near original specification as possible.

The superstructure was also completely rebuilt including steel engine room bulkhead with doors to the hold, which has a full set of false floors, running planks, box mast, stands, cratch etc. and black side and top cloths, with securing ropes. The cabin superstructure was also built in traditional style, the interior with folding cross bed, drop down table, side bed, stove bench, cast iron bottle stove, cupboards, drawers etc. The exterior is of 1/2in. sheathing boards over 1 1/4in tongued and grooved boards and oak framings with felt sheathing, oak handrails, doors and sliding hatch.

Engine room details include the Muir & Findlay riveted steel scotch return tube, coal fired boiler, 5ft diameter x 5ft long, built 1928, Maker's No. 13813, which was retubed in 1974, hydraulic tested 23/4/74 to 150psi, steam tested to 100psi, September 1982, with fittings including twin water gauges with glass gauge protectors, and shut off cocks, pressure gauge, twin Turnbull safety valves, main stop, blower, whistle, injector, ejector, clack and blow down valves and washout plugs. The engine is a twin cylinder simple vertical 'A' frame marine unit of circa 1910, with brass bound mahogany lagged cylinders, 4 1/2" bore x 6" stroke, drain cocks and pipework, displacement lubricator, lever and quadrant operated Stephenson's link reversing, counter balanced crankshaft with drip lubricators to three main bearings and coupled to 2 1/2" diameter tubular steel shaft with three bladed bronze propeller 31in diameter x 43in pitch.

Further engine room equipment includes a Worthington Simpson Duplex feed pump, a Hall single cylinder bulk head mounted feed pump, injector, bilge ejector, feed water heat exchanger, mud separator, two tone whistle, communication bell, oil cans, spanners etc. and twin coal bunkers.

The Vessel comes equipped with navigational equipment, mooring and towing ropes, mooring pins, masthead lamp etc. The hull is finished in black with black sheets and white lettering, the superstructure in multi-coloured period decorations and lettered Fellows, Morton & Clayton Ltd., 1396 'President' No. 195. The boatman's cabin interior is oak grained with red mouldings and the engine room interior red, blue and partially oak grained.

The 'President', built at Saltley, Birmingham in 1909, was used on the 'fly' service between London, Birmingham, Leicester and Nottingham. The original steam plant was removed in 1925, and she was finally sold by Fellows, Morton & Clayton Ltd. in 1944. The present owners acquired her in 1973 in sinking condition and rebuilt her over 5 years at a cost in excess of £20,000. She is the last ex-Fellows, Morton & Clayton Ltd., steam powered canal barge in existence, reconstructed as nearly as possible to the original, and is offered, subject to survey, lying at Norton Canes.

The owners undertake to complete the annual repaint which will be commenced in October, 1982."

Again, there were no takers.

New Owners & Boiler
(1982 - 1990)

At the Christie's auction on 25th October 1982, *President* failed to meet the reserve set, but an earlier bid of £19,000 was accepted, and the Black Country Museum (as it was called then) and West Midlands County Council became the joint owners of the boat. The bid was made up of a £15,000 contribution from the West Midlands County Council, £4.000 from the Science Museum in London, and the Black Country Museum agreeing to pay the maintenance and running costs.

Councillor David Sparks from West Midlands County Council and Ian Walden, director of the Black Country Museum. (Photo: unknown)

In 1983, the boat made only one outing from the Black Country Museum. In October she went to Stourbridge and back. Over the winter of 1983/84, as a result of the 10 year boiler inspection, the boiler had to be removed and sent away for re-tubing and ultrasonic testing. After the successful refitting of the boiler and steam testing, *President* was ready for her first visit to an IWA National Rally under the new ownership.

(*Photo: M. Parker*)

This trip was sponsored by the brewery Mitchells & Butlers, and the butty *Northwich* had an M & B cargo of hop sacks and barrels of beer loaded into the hold and towed to Hawkesbury Junction, the venue for the rally. The crew were also treated to free food and drink in the evenings at M & B pubs on the way.

In October 1984, 'Friends of President' was launched at County Hall in Birmingham, with a committee being formed by December, from the available membership. Friends of President was created to support the museum in the operation and maintenance of the boat.

The work done during this first winter included replacing the counter deck sheering planks, the deck cants and the ash strips that are fitted onto the cants. A new cabin stove top pipe was needed as well as work in the engine hole, which included modification to the safety valve blast pipe and flexible exhaust pipe, and re-plumbing to the Worthington pump exhaust.

There was an early start to cruising in 1985, with the boat taking part in the Icicle Cruise to Parkhead towards the end of March. Parkhead is at the other end of Dudley tunnel from the museum, but because she was too big to traverse the tunnel, *President* had to leave the museum and head in the other direction, go down Factory locks onto the new main line, then travel through Netherton tunnel and round to Parkhead using the Dudley No 2 Canal.

As well as various training runs for the new crew, the boat also attended events around the Birmingham area, such as the BCNS Rally at Titford Pools, the Science Museum Traction Engine Rally halfway down Farmers Bridge locks, the Birmingham Boating Festival at Cambrian Wharf and the Galton Valley Rally. The cruising year ended with a trip to the Bonded Warehouse at Stourbridge in September.

In November she was towed to Caggy's Boatyard, about half a mile from the bottom of Factory locks and put on their dry dock for inspection. It was found that there was one rotted board which needed replacing. New bolts were fitted, the joints were caulked and the new board spiked to the keelson. The shoe plating (tingling) was renewed on both sides where the docking baulks allowed; these are the large timbers across the bottom of the dock on which the boat rests.

The engine was also given an overhaul. New pivot pins were put in the valve gear and new sliding quadrant gear locks were fitted. The steam chest cover bolts were replaced and the slide valves were refaced. Finally, the big ends were taken up and scraped to the crankshaft, and new phosphor bronze little ends were made with some modifications.

In March 1986, the West Midlands County Council was abolished, and their share of the boat passed to Dudley Metropolitan Borough Council.

In May, after all the work had been completed, *President* had another trip to the Birmingham Science Museum. This was followed at the end of June with another visit to Caggy's yard. After this she was towed to Les Allen's boatyard at Valencia Wharf for work to be carried out on the cabin, which included new

Caggy's yard.(Photo: M. Parker)

cabin sides and roof sheathing, all the cabin metalwork being shot blasted, new styling boards and handrails being fitted and new slides made for the hatches. Finally the painting and signwriting was renewed.

All of this work was completed by the beginning of August, in time for the start of the trip to the IWA National Festival, which, in 1986, was being held at Brentford. This trip was sponsored by Heldite. On the way through Stoke Bruerne she again picked up the butty *Northwich*, which accompanied *President* to the Festival and then returned with her to the Black Country Museum. The final trip of the year was again to the Bonded Warehouse at Stourbridge.

Brentford (Photo: M. Parker)

Gloucester (Photo: M. Parker)

1987 was a busier year for the boat. Following the routine winter maintenance and boiler inspection, she attended three events around Birmingham (the Titford 150 rally, a Science Museum gathering and the BWB Pageant), followed by a trip to Ellesmere Port for a festival there. All of this took place in May. July saw *President* towing the butty *Northwich* to its new home outside the British Waterways Museum at Gloucester Docks, and then returning in time to set off for the IWA National Rally, which was again being held at Hawkesbury Junction. The year ended with the now regular trip to Stourbridge.

May 1988 saw the boat heading to Brierley Hill, and then on to the Ellesmere Port Festival. On the way back the boat stopped for a few days at Norbury Junction so that it could be surveyed in the dry dock there. There was a trip to Leamington Spa before the longer trip to the IWA National Boat Rally & Carnival. Castlefields (Manchester) was the host to this year's event, which gave the opportunity for a trip along the Manchester Ship Canal from Ellesmere Port. *Vulcan*, another FMC ex-steamer, now fitted with a Lister JP2 engine, was *President*'s escort.

The return from Castlefields, after another voyage along the ship canal, was via Stourbridge for a gathering of FMC boats, before returning to the Museum. The final long trip of the year was to a festival at Nottingham.

As a result of the survey carried out at Norbury earlier in the year, *President* was docked at the Black Country Museum in October, where the engine and boiler were removed, as was the cabin. The bottom boards under the engine and boiler area needed to be replaced. In addition to this, the 60 year old boiler, which had been re-tubed in 1974, and again in 1984, failed its inspection.

The boiler failed the inspection. (Photo: N. Oliver)

President remained on the boat dock at the Museum for the whole of 1989 whilst the partial re-bottoming was carried out. In July, the first new board was fitted. As all of the boards were being replaced towards the stern of the boat, the new boards were fitted working from the existing boards towards the stern. The width of each board was dependent on the position of the chine bolts that held it in place. Each board was offered up to the preceding one and planed if necessary. The top inch of the boards face exactly, but the bottom two inches had a lead planed into them so that they could be caulked.

The boards were drilled from above, through the existing chine bolt holes. 5/8 inch galvanised bolts were used, with the nut at the chine end. The drill used was slightly undersize, and the underside was countersunk by an inch. The board would wear with use, and this inch of timber would gradually disappear. The bolt had an oakum grommet put round its head before it was fitted. Once drilled, the ends of the boards were marked and were cut back so that they were ¾ inch proud of the hull side. Some boat builders prefer to cut all the boards in place afterwards, but those on *President* were trimmed on the bank, just before they were fitted. The excess width allowed for wear over the years, as the edge would often touch the bottom, and ensured that the chine bolt holes were not too close to the end of the board. The gap between the board and the chine was caulked with oakum, and then sealed with hot pitch.

The aft twelve feet of the keelson also needed replacing and this was done after all the boards had been fitted. A three feet long scarfed joint was made between the old and the new keelsons. The boards were then bolted onto the keelson using half inch galvanised bolts, with nuts countersunk into the top of the keelson. The bottom was then caulked, the boat being jacked up on two bostocks which enabled it to be tilted over to make the job easier. The oakum had to be drawn out and rolled into strands, and then hammered into the joints with a caulking iron - a wide bladed chisel with a groove to hold the oakum in position while it was being driven. The process was repeated until the oakum was tightly packed into the joint, three rows of oakum being used in each joint. When caulked, the ends of the elm bottoms were tingled with tinplate. The tingling covered the outer 6 inches of the underneath of the bottom boards and wrapped around to protect the ends.

A new boiler was ordered from Cochran's of Annan. This new boiler would differ from the old one in two respects. Firstly it would be of reduced diameter, more akin to those originally fitted in the steamers.

Secondly, the boiler being removed was a wet back one, whereas the replacement was a dry back. In a wet back boiler the rear face of the combustion chamber is totally surrounded by water, whereas in a dry back boiler the combustion chamber is a brick lined unit situated at the rear of the water space. This simplifies construction but does reduce the efficiency.

Two methods of clearing the propeller before the weed hatch was fitted. (Photos: M. Parker)

The gunwales were replaced, and a weed hatch was fitted, and the hull was repainted inside and out. In November, with all of the out of water work being finished, the boat was put back into its natural environment. Work could now commence installing everything again. The new boiler was craned into the boat in March 1990. The new canvas side cloths were delivered and fitted, a new fore end hatch was made and the fore end oak cants were replaced.

In April, the smoke box arrived, the cabin above the boiler was moved forward and the smoke box installed. The ceramic lining for the return box at the rear of the boiler was fitted by the contractors. The cabin had to be extended by nine inches to accommodate the new boiler and a further seven inches to create more safety space around the engine, which had been rebuilt and reconditioned. The cabin above the boiler was bolted in place and the roof tack welded. The cratch and shortened top planks were erected and covered with a new set of cloths. By the end of April 1990, the boat was ready to set off on its trip to London.

The Brindley Trust had commissioned a statue of James Brindley, to be erected on a plinth at Etruria, at the junction of the Caldon Canal with the Trent & Mersey Canal. The Black Country Museum was asked if *President* could carry the statue from London to Etruria. On the way south, the boat stopped off at Little Venice for the Canalway Cavalcade event which is held every year over the early May Bank Holiday weekend.

After the weekend *President* travelled to Limehouse Basin and then via the tidal Thames to St Katherine's Dock, where the statue of James Brindley was lowered into the hold. Whilst a section of the covers remained open so that the statue could be seen, the Trust advised that it was considered unlucky if the statue was fully displayed before its official unveiling. A white cloth was draped over the statue, leaving only the head and shoulders visible.

The route to be taken with the statue was up the River Thames to Oxford, then the whole length of the Oxford Canal to Hawkesbury Junction, where a detour *Loading the statue. (Photo: M. Parker)* was to be made into Coventry Basin for a civic reception with the Mayor of Coventry. Unfortunately, the Mayor was kept waiting for over an hour because the weed growing in the Coventry Canal delayed the progress of the boat. There were frequent stops to clear the propeller on *President* and the accompanying crew boat, *Vulcan*. A British Waterway's tug towed both boats the majority of the way. By the time of the arrival in Coventry, the statue was sporting a red neckerchief and flat cap.

From Coventry, the route was up to Fradley Junction and on to the Trent & Mersey Canal to Great Haywood. Here a short excursion was made down the Staffs & Worcs Canal to Tixall Wide. This meant that the statue made at least a visit to most of the canals James Brindley built in his Grand Plan. By the time the boat arrived at its destination at Etruria, the various crews of *President* were well acquainted with the statue, or 'Jimmy' as he became known, because the only place that the chemical toilet could be placed was at his feet!

The statue was safely delivered and erected on the plinth. *President* returned to Etruria for the official unveiling a month later. She collected the dignitaries, including the Mayor of Stoke-on-Trent and Lord Hesketh, the Minister of State in the Department of Trade and Industry, from Longport Wharf and delivered them to the garden where the statue stood on its plinth. Lord Hesketh unveiled the statue.

Brindley at Etruria.(Photo: R. Thomas)

The Friends of President received a plaque (pictured left), with the following inscription:-

Presented By The James Brindley Memorial Committee To The Friends Of President In Appreciation For The Transportation Of The James Brindley Statue London To Stoke-on-Trent 1990

(Photo: K. Rogers)

The trips in 1990 finished with a visit to Gloucester Docks for the IWA National Festival in August. The chance was taken to visit the end of the of the Stroudwater Canal, where *President* was photographed with the fore end resting on the bridge that was the first obstruction on the canal.

Stroudwater Canal. (Photo: M. Parker)

The return trip was made via Worcester and Stourport. Finally, there was a visit to the Boater's Gathering at Windmill End, situated at the southern end of Netherton Tunnel.

Another winter of maintenance work was carried out by the volunteers of Friends of President. This year there were planned changes to the engine room which required the removal of part of the cabin. When the boat was restored, an 1899 vintage Worthington Simpson water feed pump had been installed but in 1988 this was exchanged for a more modern unit which was of 1920's or 1930's manufacture. This pump was removed and sent for reconditioning.

The main steam valve was modified. All the valves were fitted with new seatings. A new funnel was fitted which incorporated a discharge pipe that sat over the safety valve outlet, so that the valve blowing off would no longer pull a draught over the fire. With the design of the new boiler, it was not possible to use the original safety valve discharge pipe. A cracked valve chest cover was replaced. A coal bunker was fitted on the starboard side. Most of the bunker was along the bottom of the boat, with a chute from the cabin roof. It held about seven bags of coal and discharged at floor level to the right of the boiler.

The bilge ejector valve was replaced and relocated. The filter box lid was strengthened, and a 12 volt bilge pump was installed under the cabin floor, with a float switch which would automatically activate the pump. Parts of the boat needing attention were repainted. The cloths were blacked and the white lettering reapplied.

President entered 1991 ready for new adventures.

1973 - President (right) at Hayhurst Yard, Northwich. (Photo: R. Thomas)

1977 - Ready for re-floating at Norton Canes. (Photo: N. Bostock)

1978 - First test on the Cannock Extension.
(Photo: N. Bostock)

1978 - Approaching Coseley Tunnel.
(Photo: N. Bostock)

1979 - Entering the Manchester Ship Canal at Ellesmere Port. (Photo: N. Bostock)

1978 – Leaving the IWA National Rally of Boats at Titford Pools. (Photo: N. Oliver)

1979 – Moored at Audlem en route to Ellesmere Port. (Photo: N. Bostock)

1979 – Arriving at the IWA National Rally at Northwich. (Photo: R. Prior)

1980 – Moored at Camden on the return from Walthamstow. (Photo: N. Bostock)

1983 – At the Black Country Museum. (Photo: N. Oliver)

1986 – Returning from the Bonded Warehouse, Stourbridge. (Photo: M. Parker)

1987 – Passing through Chester after a festival at Ellesmere Port. (Photo: M. Parker)

1987 – Upton upon Severn, taking Northwich to Gloucester. (Photo: N. Ratcliffe)

1989 – On the dock at the Black Country Museum. (Photo: N. Oliver)

1990 – The statue of James Brindley on board at Coventry Basin. (Photo: N. Ratcliffe)

1991 – Crossing Wolverton Aqueduct during the first fly run. (Photo: R. Thomas)

1991 – Sarah & Richard Poole outside the Admiral Nelson at Braunston. (Photo: M. Parker)

1992 – First trip with Kildare, from Warwickshire Fly Boats to Coventry. (Photo: M. Parker)

1992 – Leaving Etruria during the Big Food Run. (Photo: R. & J. Spencer)

1996 – Transporting IWA branch jigsaw pieces. (Photo: R. & J. Spencer)

1999 - 90th Birthday Cake presented at Gas Street Basin. (Photo: N. Oliver)

2001 – New elm boards and tingling. (Photo: B. Empsall)

2001 – New stern end taking shape. (Photo: B. Empsall)

2003 – Entering the water after the second restoration. (Photo: R. & J. Spencer)

2003 – Ascending Delph Locks after completion of the restoration. (Photo: S. Nuttall)

2003 – Returning from the Bonded Warehouse, Stourbridge. (Photo: S. Nuttall)

2005 – Arriving at Stoke Bruerne at the end of the 5th fly run. (Photo: R. Prior)

2005 – Outside the Floatel Hotel on the River Weaver at Northwich with Malcolm Braine's Cactus. (Photo: R. & J. Spencer)

2005 – Above and below the Anderton Boat Lift. A detour onto the River Weaver on the way to Preston Brook. (Photos: J.A. Oldfield)

2007 – At the head of navigation on the Ashby Canal. (Photo: B. Empsall)

2008 – Outside Billing Aquadrome on the River Nene. (Photo: B. Empsall)

2008 – Leaving Salter's Lode on the Middle Level. (Photo: N. Oliver)

2008 – Guests at the Netherton 150 celebrations. (Photo: B. Empsall)

Fly Runs & Fusible Plugs
(1991 - 1999)

With all the costs involved with maintaining a steam powered narrow boat, another role for the Friends of President was required, that of fundraising. The suggestion of recreating a fly run to raise money was enthusiastically accepted. The original start time and change over points would be used but extra time would be allowed to compensate for the shallower state of the canal and the change in acceptable boating techniques.

Thus 1991 saw the first fly run for *President* since its original steamer days, running from London City Road Basin to Braunston, with two four-man crews exchanging shifts every 4½ hours, arriving the evening

Setting off for London. (Photo: N. Oliver)

before the Braunston Boat Show opened. The off duty crew were accommodated on an accompanying boat, again the ex-steamer *Vulcan*.

On arrival at Braunston top lock the crews were given two messages, firstly to take their time, because they were early, and secondly, that there was a lady outside the Admiral Nelson who had some old photos of *President*. The lady turned out to be Mrs Sarah Poole, the daughter of James Woodfield, *President*'s first Captain. One of the photographs was of her father (see page 17).

Another was the missing 'Buckby' picture taken in 1911, with her father at the tiller (see below).

PRESIDENT above lock 11 at Buckby
(Woodfield family)

The remaining photograph was a complete version of the original image we had of *President* which had been torn in half.

At last the whole picture was available. Sarah identified the young man sitting on the roof as her brother Jimmy Woodfield, and the man standing in the engine hole as her uncle Sam Woodfield, although she did not know the name of the steerer (or the dog!).

After a short stop with the Woodfields, the boats moved slowly to the bottom lock, where they were joined by two students from Sheffield who were carrying the World Student Games Flame. This flame was being taken from Sapporo, in Japan, where the Winter Student Games were held, to Sheffield. This journey had taken the flame via America and Canada. *President* was now carrying it for the few hundred yards from the bottom lock to Braunston Marina. (The flame would later be carried again from Gas Street Basin to the International Convention Centre in Birmingham where the International Olympic Committee was meeting).

The bank was lined with people, there were hundreds of flashes from cameras and when the boats arrived at the Marina entrance the Town Crier welcomed them. They were then treated to a large firework display together with the 1812 Overture playing over the loudspeakers. The bells of Braunston Church were ringing up on the hill. It was a fitting

End of the fly run. (Photo: M. Parker)

finale to the trip. Money had been raised by individuals and companies sponsoring a lock on the route, together with land based volunteers collecting donations as the boats passed. It proved to be very successful.

1991 was also the year when the Black Country Museum became the sole owner of *President*.

Other trips for the year were to Ellesmere Port, Etruria, Birmingham, Stone Cross on the Tame Valley Canal, the IWA National Festival at Windmill End, and Stourbridge. Fifteen members of the Woodfield family, covering three generations, were entertained at the Museum in September. Then it was time for the winter maintenance program again. February 1992 saw the boat once again on the dry dock at Caggy's boatyard. A new propeller shaft was fitted with a substantial bracket and bearing just aft of the engine. Twenty four feet of tingling was replaced, and the sides were blacked.

The ex-steamer *Vulcan* had acted as the crew boat for *President* on a few trips. Other members' boats had also been used, *Myndynawr*, *Brunel*, and *Sir Daniel Gooch*. In the early days of the Friends a number of Brummagem Boats hire craft were used when they were based at Sherborne Street in Birmingham. Two years previously, in 1990, the decision had been taken to buy the FMC Braithwaite-built butty, *Kildare*, to act as the crew boat. The winter period saw a lot of work in converting this boat into a suitable companion for *President*.

First trip with Kildare. (Photo: M. Parker)

President travelled to Warwickshire Fly Boats on the Grand Union Canal at Stockton in March for a repaint and to be introduced to her new travelling companion. The maiden voyage of the pair was to Calcutt Locks on April 11th 1992, fourteen years to the day after *President*'s maiden voyage as a restored steamer. This was followed by a trip to Coventry and back to the Museum.

The main event of 1992 was the Big Food Run. It took place in May and June and the object was to collect tinned food for the St Laurence Children's Hospice at Cernavoda in Romania. It was held in conjunction with the charity Romania's Childrens' Aid and the British Red Cross.

Some of the food collected. (Photo: S. Nuttall)

President and *Kildare* started this run at Ellesmere Port and travelled along the Shropshire Union Canal to Barbridge, across to Middlewich, down the Trent & Mersey Canal to Great Haywood, along the Staffs & Worcs Canal to Aldersley Junction, and up the Wolverhampton 21 to the Museum. Then they went through

Birmingham and down the Grand Union Canal to Little Venice. The boats stopped at various places to act as the focal point where people could deliver food. At various pre-arranged points on the route these donations were collected from the boats by lorry. A total of over 650 boxes of tinned food were collected, with an estimated weight of 7 tons, and a value of £10,000, and sent to Romania. It had turned out to be a very worthwhile use of the boats.

Other events attended in 1992 were at the Birmingham Science Museum, Upton-on-Severn, Worcester, Nottingham and Stourbridge.

Over the winter period the boiler passed the annual inspection. For the first time since installation, the longitudinal weld of the boiler was exposed, examined ultrasonically and found to be sound. The badly situated blow down valve was moved to a more accessible position. Klinger prismatic water gauges were fitted to replace the existing ones. The engine was fitted with new gudgeon pins, and new drip feed oilers to feed the bottom ends. The rudder was removed, repaired and replaced. It was another very busy time for the volunteers who turn up for the regular working parties that are held during the non-cruising periods.

In 1993 there were trips to the Canalway Cavalcade at Little Venice, the Rickmansworth Festival and then back to London for the start of the second fly run. The first part of this was to Braunston, and the second was the onward journey to Gas Street Basin. After this there were visits to Etruria and Windmill End.

Rickmansworth. (Photo: R. & J. Spencer)

At the end of the cruising season, the engine was removed for rebuilding. January to March was spent at the British Waterways workshop at Bradley while the canal arm at the museum and the section of canal to Dudley Tunnel were drained for maintenance. The boat was put on the dock and surveyed, with no problems being found.

It was not until June 1994 that the engine was reinstalled in the boat and everything was tested. Following a visit to the Bratch locks in July, the boats were returning to the museum via the Wolverhampton 21 when water was spotted running out of the ash pit. A leaking fusible plug was suspected.

The purpose of the plug is to protect the furnace tube from overheating due to a low water level in the boiler. If the water level is allowed to fall so that the furnace tube, in which the fire is held, becomes uncovered, the rise in temperature will be so great that the tube could distort leading to a failure of the boiler. To protect the furnace tube a plug, containing lead, is screwed into the furnace tube above the fire from the fire side. Should the water level fall and the tip of the plug become exposed, the temperature will quickly rise, melting the lead, and allow a jet of steam to douse the fire, thereby protecting the furnace tube.

The fusible plug fitted to *President*'s boiler is a one inch long tapered plug screwed into a parallel threaded socket two inches wide by two inches long, which is welded into the furnace tube above the fire. This plug is replaced each year as part of the routine maintenance.

If a leaking fusible plug is suspected, the driver would feed cold water into the boiler and draw the fire onto the floor plates in the engine room. However, the boiler gauge glasses indicated that the water level in the boiler was correct. After the boat was towed back to the museum, the plug was removed and sent for analysis to the boiler manufacturer's laboratories at Derby. They found no reason, other than low water level, why the plug should have operated.

In the meantime the boat was committed to attend the 1994 IWA National Festival at Waltham Abbey. A new plug was fitted and *President* set off to London. The first plug had blown after approximately 35 hours steaming, and more or less on the dot the second plug blew. Again there was nothing wrong with the water level in the boiler. The boat had reached Leighton Buzzard when the third plug was detected on the point of failure.

The plug is screwed into the bottom of the socket from the fire side of the furnace tube. The body of the plug is approximately one inch long which leaves a space above the plug in the socket. To see if this was the problem, it was decided to fit a long nosed plug which would extend through the socket into the water space above. However, it was not possible to fit this type of plug because the nose would not go through the socket. It was meeting an obstruction. When a screw driver was pushed up into the hole, it dislodged a lump of scale that had formed in the top of the socket. The tip of the plug had been shielded by the scale and, starved of water, had slowly come up to the melt point. An old type of plug was again fitted and the boat went off to London and Waltham Abbey without any further problems.

Safety regulations demand that the pressure plate and furnace tube welds are inspected every five years. To enable an inspector to examine these welds the boiler has to be lifted from the boat and all the cladding removed. At the end of January 1995, *President* was towed to the British Waterways workshop at Bradley so that this could be carried out. With the boiler out, the safety valve was moved forward of the steam dome, giving easier access for maintenance and enabling the steam to go up the blast pipe instead of the funnel. The back water gauge was also moved to its correct position on the left hand side of the boiler.

Bradley. (Photo: M. Parker)

In 1995, the boat was unable to travel anywhere until later in the year due to more problems with the boiler. She attended the IWA National Festival in Chester, followed by a trip to Ellesmere Port before returning to the Museum.

1996 was the year that the Inland Waterways Association celebrated its Golden Jubilee. The Hertfordshire Branch had co-sponsored, with British Waterways, some souvenir glasses. *President* and *Kildare* had the honour of carrying these glasses from the Nazeing Glassworks on the Lee Navigation back to Birmingham, via the Canalway Cavalcade at Little Venice where they would also be on sale. Every branch of the IWA also commissioned a jigsaw piece. The whole jigsaw would then be assembled in Birmingham as part of the World Canal Conference in June. Throughout the early part of the year the boats collected various jigsaw pieces from different IWA branches.

Sonia Rolt. (Photo: M. Parker)

Rickmansworth Canal Festival was attended after Little Venice, and then it was back to City Road for the start of *President*'s third fly run, which would end at Braunston in time for the Boat Show. From Braunston the boats went to Etruria, and then back to Birmingham to deliver the eight jigsaw pieces that had been collected on the boat's travels. The year's cruising ended with the IWA National Festival at Windmill End and a trip to the Ashby Canal for the Shackerstone Steam Festival. On the way to Shackerstone, Sonia Rolt joined the crew for a section of the journey along the Ashby Canal.

Events attended in 1997 were at Merry Hill, Wolverhampton, Gloucester, Nottingham & Leicester.

In 1998 the boats visited Braunston, and once again travelled the Manchester Ship Canal on their way to Salford Quays for the IWA National Festival.

A full lock on the Manchester Ship Canal. (Photo: M. Parker)

Early in 1999, before the first outing, *President* was docked at Bradley to investigate some slow leaks around the counter. A considerable amount of corrosion was found and it was decided that before very long the whole of the swim and counter would have to be replaced, together with a large number of bottom boards.

The fourth fly run was planned for 1999, this time from Birmingham to Braunston, arriving in time for the Braunston Boat Show. A video of this trip was made by S.K. Productions. Footage was also shot by the BBC for the Songs Of Praise TV programme. The opening

Non stop fly run! (Photo: N. Oliver)

shots for the programme were filmed at Calcutt, but more than one take was required which didn't go down too well with other boaters, held up behind. Filming continued much of the way to Braunston, along the Grand Union Canal. Later in the year, a trip to the Waterways Museum at Gloucester was coupled with, on the return journey, attendance at the IWA National Festival at Worcester.

Second Restoration
(2000 - 2008)

The survey at Bradley in 1999 had highlighted the serious deterioration of the original rivets and plate work of the swim, counter and stern section, and plans were now being made for a major renovation of all of these areas, plus the cabin and a complete re-bottoming for *President* at Ian Kemp's yard at Dadford's Shed on the Stourbridge flight of locks. The work was scheduled to start in the winter of 2000.

Meanwhile, there were still trips to be made during the year. These included visits to Etruria, Middlewich and Birmingham. There was also a Midsummer Steam Evening at the Black Country Living Museum with Fred Dibnah in attendance, when he walked around in the pouring rain, signing autographs and chatting to the visitors.

The engine that had been installed by Malcolm Braine during the first restoration was now getting tired and wasn't powerful enough now that a butty was regularly being towed. The existing engine was a long way from the type fitted to the FMC steamer fleet, so in trying to be as authentic as possible serious consideration had been given to building a replica of the original Haines engine. By using a full set of drawings of a tunnel tug engine, kindly donated by the Waterways Museum at Gloucester, an engineer volunteered to design and build such an engine. He produced a full set of external drawings, but sadly due to ill health the project had to be abandoned.

So a search began for a replacement engine. This search ended at Preston Steam in Canterbury where a virtually unused unit was found. The new engine was built by Sissons, in around 1954 as a training engine for a Merchant Navy Training College to teach the principles of steam. It was single cylinder, with a 7 inch bore and 12 inch stroke, capable of producing 15 hp at 175 rpm at 150 psi, and would meet all the power requirements. The engine was purchased together with a suitable condenser for £7750. Preston Steam fitted hard wood lagging to the cylinder and painted the frame dark green leaving all the motion in bright steel.

he new Sissons engine. (Photo: B. Empsall)

Delivered by Sentinel steam lorry to the IWA National Festival. (Photo: R. Thomas)

The last journey using the old engine was to Waltham Abbey for the IWA National Festival and it was there that the new engine was delivered by a Sentinel steam lorry. A large crane was waiting to load it carefully into the hold. President then returned to Dudley carrying its new engine.

January 27th 2001 saw *President* being towed to Ian Kemp's yard by *Enterprise*, which in an earlier life had been the ex-FMC steamer *Count*. The engine and boiler had already been removed. She was lifted out onto the bank and completely stripped down to the bare hull.

Blanking plate shown on boat and after removal. (Photos: R. Thomas)

When *President* was converted to a diesel engine in 1925, the cabin was shortened and the blanking plate, shown above left, replaced the original forward bulkhead angle of the boiler cabin. This section of plating was renewed in the second restoration but the original was preserved in the archives. The rear section of the hull, from the front of the cabin to the stern, was fully renovated and included a new swim area. All the bottom boards were replaced with elm sourced in Scotland. All the restoration work copied the 1909 original wherever possible.

A major problem was the supply of the rubbing strips that surround the hull. The size was non standard, but a local rolling mill agreed to do a special run. A new and improved weed hatch assembly was fitted. The forward hatch area was in a sorry state, the frame which holds the bulkhead in place, was corroded. The shoe plate, which sits below the bow, was also corroded, so this was replaced. The hatch was de-scaled and coated with red oxide. The whole of the hull was shot blasted. The outside was coated with a two-part epoxy resin and the inside with red oxide.

New stern end. (Photo: M. Parker)

Boiler cabin. (Photo: B. Empsall)

The back cabin was rebuilt with a new metal cabin over the boiler. A new design was used for the front of the boiler cabin. The cabin over the boiler was originally designed to be removable, but doing this would have risked distorting it and would have broken the weather seal every time it was removed. In the changed design, the top and sides were fixed and the forward bulkhead and doors were made removable instead. The boiler would now be able to slide out on greased rails into the hold. The doors would also help to keep the coal dust away from the blow down valve and other valves at the forward end of the boiler.

After research, and in the interest of safety, two sliding hatches were fitted to make access to the engine hole easier. The existing smoke box was reduced in height to enable it to clear the cabin supports, and the funnel with its hinged mounting was mounted on a removable plate, the underside of which was extended down to meet the top of the smoke box.

The boiler being taken away for inspection. (Photo: B. Empsall)

The boiler was taken to Thompson's boiler works at Oldham as it was due for its second five year inspection. All the lagging was removed and the welded seams ultrasonically tested. The boiler passed its inspection and was returned to Stourbridge to await its re-installation.

Consideration was now given to the possibility of running condensing, as the original steamers did. The original engine had a jet condenser fitted to the engine frame. This is a simple box with an upper and lower compartment. Exhaust steam enters the upper part where it meets a water spray that condenses it back to water also producing a vacuum, which increases the efficiency of the engine. The lower part has a ram pump which sucks the water and any air through disc valves and ejects the water back into the canal.

To design and build a jet condenser was considered too expensive so it was decided to incorporate the surface condenser purchased with the engine. This is a cylinder capped at both ends through which pass a number of copper tubes. The ends of the tubes are enclosed inside a further cap. Cold water is pumped into one end through the tubes and out the other end back into the cut. The exhaust steam is admitted into the cavity surrounding the tubes, where on striking the cold tubes, it condenses back to water creating a partial vacuum. This water, called condensate, is then sucked out by a pump, which also increases the vacuum, which again improves the efficiency of the engine and also eliminates the exhaust beat (the chuffing sound). Neither *President*, nor any other steamer in the fleet exhausted up the funnel, although they were fitted with a diverter valve; they all ran virtually silently.

President, since its first restoration, has always run with the exhaust up the funnel producing the chuff chuff sound that is now expected by all. This becomes a major problem in tunnels as the steam from the funnel can block all forward vision; this is now eliminated by changing over to running condensing.

The next problem was how to circulate cold water through the condenser and extract the water and air. Marine steam plants use two pumps driven by the engine. Suitable pumps could be found at a cost, but there was very limited space. The decision was made to use ejectors, a large one to circulate the cooling water and a small one to pull the air and water. They work well although they are a bit greedy with steam.

Because the old engine ran ahead anti-clockwise and the new one ahead clockwise, a new propeller was needed. This was manufactured by a specialist company in Holland. The new blade has a diameter of 34 inches and a pitch of approximately 42 inches.

The new propeller. (Photo: R. & J. Spencer)

Getting ready for the lift off the dockside....

... and back safely in the water. (Photos: B. Empsall)

A large mobile crane was brought to Dadford's Shed and positioned on the dockside. It was to be used to lift the restored hull, weighing 12.5 tonnes, complete with its new cabin but without any machinery, back into the water. The occasion was marked with much ceremony and a bottle of champagne.

(Lifting the engine and boiler into the boat. (Photos: B. Empsall)

A smaller crane was used to lift the new engine and the refurbished boiler into the boat.

The first steaming. (Photo: S. Nuttall)

Saturday 22nd February 2003 saw the first steaming of *President* since the autumn of 2000, almost 30 months. Just over a month later, on the 29th March, *President* returned to the Black Country Living Museum under her own power.

In June, in the first major outing since the refit, *President* went to Middlewich for the Folk & Boat Festival. From there she travelled down to Braunston Marina, where *President* and *Kildare* took pride of place at the Fellows, Morton & Clayton Rally & Canal Festival.

Opening the show was Zita Sattar, 'Casualty' TV programme actress, but perhaps more importantly on this occasion, the great-great-granddaughter of the first captain, James Woodfield. Her parents and grandmother also attended, three generations of the Woodfield family.

The IWA National Festival was held at Beale Park on the River Thames and in August the boats attended this event over the Bank Holiday weekend. They returned to the museum via the Oxford Canal and Braunston and made a final trip of the year to Stourbridge in September.

Ever since the new engine was first connected to the propeller shaft there had been a knock. After much trial and error and seeking advice, the sound was traced to the stern tube bushes. *President* was docked in November 2003 and the stern tube and propeller shaft were removed. New bushes and a new tail shaft were made. A new connection was fabricated which used an expanding insert to join the two shafts together. This was fitted using a new thrust bearing. In addition, seals were put in to prevent the loss of grease and the ingress of water and silt into the sleeves. This cured the knock, but there was now a rattle!

A detailed inspection showed that this new noise was coming from the Hardy Spicer joints and splines. The speed of the engine and the resistance of the propeller were creating an imbalance, and this was causing the propeller shaft to rattle. It was felt that the flywheel was too small, so a larger one weighing about 3cwt was found and fitted. The rattle disappeared.

2004 started with a trip to Little Venice for the Canalway Cavalcade, which was followed by a week moored outside the London Canal Museum. The return to the Black Country Living Museum was via the Thames, where *President* and *Kildare*, breasted up, led a convoy out at Limehouse and upstream to the Grand Union Canal at Brentford. In June, after visiting the Working Boat Gathering at Braunston, the boats went to Foxton and Nottingham before returning to their home mooring at the museum via the Trent & Mersey Canal.

Leaving the Burton National. (Photo: R. Prior)

The IWA National Festival was held at Burton-on-Trent and *President* carried the Mayor and Mayoress to the opening ceremony. There was a degree of concern when the Mayoress arrived wearing a pristine white suit, which was possibly not the most suitable shade for a trip on a coal-burning steamer. However, the wind was kind and she arrived without polka dot patterning.

Signpost unveiling, Huddlesford. (Photo: B. Empsall)

The final trips in this busy year were to the Shackerstone Steam Festival, the Parkhead Gathering and finally Huddlesford Junction, where the Lichfield & Hatherton Canals restoration will rejoin when it is finished.

Early in April 2005, *President* was horse drawn to Caggy's boatyard, so that Ian Kemp could work on the bow and replace some of the tingling which had ripped off the edge of the hull during the previous season. The hull was blacked with a two part epoxy coating. Some pipe work in the engine room was carried out, allowing the injector controls to be moved to a more manageable height. Main bearing lubricators were fitted at the top of the engine cylinder. *President* was then towed back to the museum by a tug.

Later that month the boiler inspector visited for the annual cold inspection both inside and outside of the boiler. Following his visit, the injector was re-fitted, together with a modified auxiliary steam pipe feed, the manhole cover in the top of the boiler was re-inserted, the safety valve

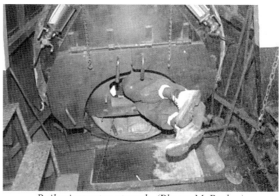

Boiler inspector at work. (Photo: M. Parker)

was re-fitted having been away for calibration, new pipe work was completed for the remounted main bearing lubricators, the cylinder drain pipe work was rerouted, the regulator handle was remounted, the big end and main bearings were inspected and refitted, new gauge glass drain pipes were fitted and finally, the engine hold down bolts were tightened.

In 2005, Nicholas Bostock commissioned an oil painting by D.C. (Dusty) Miller, the well known canal artist, of *President* and *Kildare* at the Fellows Morton & Clayton depot at Leicester. The painting was based on an original photograph of the steamer *Earl* unloading after arriving from London. President would have often unloaded at that

Dusty Miller painting. (Photo: N. Ratcliffe)

depot. Friends of President were then given exclusive rights to produce a limited edition print of the painting to be sold as part of their fundraising.

2005 was another busy year. The museum had been asked if *President* could transport three cast iron columns and two cast iron arches, all replicas of the ironwork of the original Crystal Palace. These were to be taken from the Black Country Living Museum to Greenland Dock, part of the Surrey Docks on the south bank of the Thames in London. From here they were to be taken to Upper Sydenham where they would form a token rebuilt corner of the original Crystal Palace that was re-erected there after the Great Exhibition of 1851 in Hyde Park and stood there until it was destroyed by fire in 1936.

Prior to this journey, a trip was made to Leamington for a Canal Festival, then, with the boats back at the museum, the castings were loaded into *President*'s hold. They had been well wrapped in polythene and sacking to protect them from the coal for the trip, which was then stacked on top. The boats set off for London, stopping off at the Crick Boat Show on their way.

Unloading at Greenland Dock. (Photo: N. Haynes)

The delivery to Greenland Dock meant venturing out on to the tideway at Limehouse, dodging the fast ferries on that stretch and getting safely into the dock on the south side of the river. The offloading was complemented by a delivery of coal that would be used on the return journey. The boats then re-crossed the river, locked back into Limehouse Basin, and made their way to the London Canal Museum, where they stayed until the 16th June.

On that day, *President* and *Kildare* were moved to City Road Basin ready for the fifth fly run, which was going to be slightly shorter, going only as far as Stoke Bruerne. They were scheduled to arrive there in time for the celebrations of the 200th Anniversary of Blisworth Tunnel opening. The boats stayed at Stoke Bruerne for a week and then headed to Braunston for the FMC Rally before they went back to the Black Country Living Museum.

The Severn Boat Festival was the next event, held at Worcester, with a stop on the return to attend the IWA Tardebigge Meeting, held to celebrate the 60th anniversary of the meeting of Tom Rolt and Robert Aickman that led to the formation of the IWA.

Anderton Boat Lift. (Photo: B. Empsall)

President and *Kildare* were booked to attend the IWA National Festival which was being held at Preston Brook. The opportunity was taken to make a detour down the Anderton Boat Lift onto the River Weaver at Northwich from where *President* had been rescued thirty years before. A meeting was arranged with Malcolm Braine by the Floatel Hotel, which was floating in the basin where he had first found and recognised *President*. To add to the sense of occasion, Malcolm arrived on *Cactus*, the Bolinder powered 100th motor boat built by FMC.

At the Festival opening, *President* was again used to provide transport and, in addition to the dignitaries, she carried 'Alice in Wonderland'. Lewis Carroll had been born in the nearby village of Daresbury.

Concern was mounting about the condition of *Kildare*'s hull. There seemed to be more water in the bilge than usual. The return journey to the Black Country Living Museum was interrupted by an extra stop at Dutton dry dock, just south of Preston Brook Tunnel. An inspection of *Kildare*'s hull revealed that no less than ten patches were needed to make it reasonably watertight!

After the return to the Museum, *Kildare* was docked at Caggy's yard for a full hull survey, and it was discovered that extensive repairs were required. The boat would not be available for the start of the 2006 boating programme. *Hazel Valley*, a Friend of President member's boat, was offered in its place for the run up to Middlewich for the Folk & Boat Festival, where *President* was awarded the prize for having the

'Tidiest Engine Room'. The trip continued to Ellesmere Port for the IWA Chester Branch Rally. As *President* was running single, the opportunity arose to help the Clayton tar boat *Gifford* on her way south and she was towed as far as Nantwich.

Towing Gifford from Chester. (Photo: R. Prior)

In August, as the boats were leaving the arm at the museum, setting off on their journey to Beale Park for the IWA National Festival, it was discovered that a boiler tube had failed. Sadly, this meant that the trip had to be called off. Although only one of the tubes had failed, it was decided that as they were all the same age and had lasted 15 years, it would be sensible to replace all 72 tubes.

The following year, 2008, was to be the time for the five yearly test of the boiler, when it would have to be removed from the boat. The decision was made to bring this inspection forward, which meant that if any major problems showed up during the inspection, there would be ample time to get them fixed before the centenary celebrations in 2009.

Over the winter of 2006/7, whilst waiting for the boiler to be re-tubed and refitted, other work was carried out. One aspect of a steam engine which exhausts to atmosphere is the amount of water and oil mixed with soot that leaves the funnel, and then covers the boat, the crew and any unsuspecting bystanders. A smaller problem is the noise, very pleasant when ticking over but when the engine is working hard it is very noisy. So, after consulting with other steam experts, an expansion box was designed which would alleviate both problems.

The box sits at the side of the engine. It is 42 inches high and 15 inches in diameter, insulated and clad in wood and brass to match the engine cylinder. The exhaust steam leaves the engine directly into the box where it spins round, dropping all the water and oil to the bottom where it drains out through a valve. The steam then leaves the box and goes up the funnel or to the condenser. This makes the engine run quieter and cleaner. A further modification was to fit a hand pump to clear the oil and condensate from the engine sump into a container in the hold.

With the boiler re-installed and all the other necessary work completed, the boats were ready for the 2007 boating programme. The IWA National Festival was being held on the River Great Ouse at St. Ives. *President* & *Kildare* were going to attend, making this the first time that an FMC steamer had ventured across the Middle Level and onto the Great Ouse. Various other events were also planned along the way, at Braunston, Wansford, March, Prickwillow, Ely, Cambridge, Bedford and Hartford Marina before arriving at St. Ives. T-shirts were printed with all the dates and supplied to the various crews; something that had never been done before.

Congestion during the working boat parade at Braunston. (Photo: N. Oliver)

The Historic Boat Rally at Braunston was the only event that the boats managed to attend. Heavy rain for extended periods caused the River Nene to flood and all boat movement was stopped. The pair diverted to Stoke Bruerne to wait and see whether conditions would improve. Other crewing arrangements were made, but in the end it just proved impossible for the boats to complete the planned itinerary, so they went back to the Black Country Living Museum. River levels fell but not in time to allow the boats to get to St. Ives. They attended the Shackerstone Steam Festival instead.

The Weir feed pump was becoming a major problem because the valve gear was badly worn and the conclusion was reached that infrequent use was the cause, as the pump was designed to run for long periods. To replace it, a banjo style feed pump was acquired, which is a more reliable simple rotary pump with a slide valve and a small fly wheel. The new pump was mounted on the cabin wall to replace the Weir.

When the boating programme for 2008 was being discussed, it was decided to try to fulfil last year's cancelled trip to the Middle Level and the Great Ouse, river levels permitting.

The journey started with a visit to the Waterways Festival at Foxton, and from there the boats headed for Gayton Junction and down the locks to the River Nene at Northampton. The passage of Stanground sluice in Peterborough to reach the Middle Level was accomplished with *President* going through the lock backwards. When the lock was extended to be to take 70 foot boats, the new deeper section was at the Middle Level end of the lock, so this was the only part that would take *President*'s three foot draft at the stern. This meant that she then had to be reversed for the next mile to a spot where she could be turned again.

The journey continued through the Middle Level, to the sharp Briggate bend in Whittlesey. *President* was unable to get round the bend and under the bridge which is immediately after it because there was inadequate depth. The level had to be raised by letting water through Stanground Sluice. It took three hours before there was enough water to enable her to continue.

Low bridges on Well Creek.(Photo: N. Oliver)

Waiting for a level. (Photo: N. Oliver)

After successfully negotiating Salters Lode and Denver Sluice, the boats visited the Prickwillow Drainage Museum on the River Lark, before heading for the Cam Conservators' base at Clayhythe, just north of Cambridge, which was used as a base in between other parts of the trip. *President* spent a couple of days in Cambridge, then visited the Bedford River Festival, before spending a weekend at Ely, prior to making the long return to Dudley.

A DVD was produced of the journey along the Well Creek from Marmont Priory to Salters Lode Lock by Carrillson Publications. The reproduction rights have been granted to Friends of President to help with their fundraising for *President*.

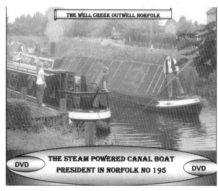

In 2008, the IWA National Festival was based around Autherley Junction, where the Shropshire Union Canal meets the Staffs & Worcs Canal. The journey down the 21 locks at Wolverhampton was unusual in that the crew did not have to bow haul *Kildare*. The Horse Boating Society borrowed a horse, Buddy, for the job. Buddy also towed *Kildare* back to the Museum from the top of the locks on the return journey.

Parkhead. (Photo: R. Prior)

The final outing of the year was to Parkhead, the return journey being via the top of the Stourbridge 16 locks, where *President* parted company with *Kildare*, which was going to Ian Kemp's yard at Stourbridge for the rebuilding of the fore cabin and a repaint. *President* returned solo to the museum.

After the work to *Kildare* had been completed, *President* then made the journey to the same yard where remedial work was carried out on the cabin. New fore end cants were fitted, as well as new ash strips to the stern end cants. The cabin was then re-painted or re-varnished where necessary.

This has been the first ninety-nine years of *President*'s life. 2009 will turn her into a centenarian. There may not be a telegram – but there will be celebrations....

A Message From David Powell
(Chairman of Friends of President)

So far in the previous chapters we have looked at the history and details of the boat. As we celebrate *President*'s centenary I feel it is important to look back on the role that the Black Country Living Museum and Friends of President have played in the preservation so far and the plans and aspirations we have to secure the future of this unique vessel.

As this book goes to print *President* is again undergoing an extensive winter maintenance programme in preparation for this year's celebrations. Some of the work is being carried out at Ian Kemp's boatyard but many jobs will involve working parties of volunteers from Friends of President. Over the past 25 years many hundreds of hours of work have been done by these volunteers. Without this commitment it is unlikely that *President* would be preserved in the format we see today.

Bow hauling President. (Photo: R. Prior)

The programme of events to mark this special year begins with a party on May 2nd at the Museum. After that weekend the boats will be taking part in a number of waterway events in many parts of the country.

Gathered for a working party. (Photo: M. Parker)

The boats don't go anywhere without crew and these are all members of Friends of President. This year's programme will require a total of 650 crewing days. The normal crew comprises a captain, a driver and four other members. We welcome anyone who is interested in crewing the boats. After attending an introduction day we encourage new members to join a trip. When asked what skills are needed, I usually reply that anyone with an interest in the canals and old boats is ideal and if you like steam it's a bonus. Over the years that Friends of President has operated the boats we have acquired a lot of skills and we are always willing to pass these on to anyone who shows an interest. I think we are also aware that we never stop learning so even the 'old' hands are constantly looking for ways to hone our skills.

Cleaning the hull. (Photo: M. Parker)

The constitution of Friends of President states that one of the main objectives of the society is to maintain and preserve *President* and *Kildare*. This is a major part of our commitment to the boats and the Museum. Working parties are held on many weekends to keep the boats in top condition and, in addition, they offer museum visitors a chance to chat and, where practical, be shown round the boats. For many this will be the highlight of their visit. In addition to maintaining the boats these days give the members the opportunity to socialise and to recall stories of yesteryear over a superb lunch from the museum's famous fish'n'chip shop.

Enjoying the fish'n'chip lunch. (Photo: B. Empsall)

So what jobs need to be done? You can name any part of a boat and at some point in its life, attention will be needed. Jobs range from scraping the bottom, blacking the hull, loading coal, and tidying the hold, to checking for leaks, re-stringing the cloths and preparation and painting.

(Photo: M. Parker)

(Photo: M. Parker)

Anyone who is a member of Friends of President can attend working parties. For newer members, working parties provide valuable knowledge and experience of the boats. There will always be someone to show you what to do and where and how to do it. If you have a particular skill that can be used, be sure that we will use it!

Learning the art of splicing. (Photo: M. Parker)

Most working parties are held at the museum on a Saturday, though if you have a distance to travel, Sundays can be included. You can stay overnight on *Kildare* or in one of the houses at the museum. Occasionally, we have outings to hold working parties at other sites – boatyards where we take the boats for major work.

Boiler maintenance has to be carried out each year to comply with the regulations. Annually the boiler is opened up and two or three buckets full of loose scale is removed from the inside of the boiler. The smoke box doors are opened and the tube plate and the tubes are cleaned. The rear door to the back combustion chamber is opened and the tube plate cleaned and all ash and coal removed from the pit. For anyone who has a predilection for getting dirty, this is a must!

The boiler is then ready for the visual examination by the surveyor. He is looking for any signs of corrosion or wasting on any of the internal surfaces. Once he is satisfied, the boiler is filled and steamed to prove all is well. The surveyor will later return and witness the formal steam test. This includes the visual examination of all boiler fittings, the blow down of the water gauges to prove they are showing the correct level of water and finally the checking of the safety valve. Provided that all is in order, the boiler is certified for another year.

Local members are encouraged to pop down to the museum for a few hours or so just to keep the boats aired and give them a little TLC, clean the brasses, light the ranges, and talk to visitors. The important thing is to enjoy it. The boats are not a chore, they are an enjoyable hobby. They are a vital link to the tradition and the history of the canals. In this centenary year it is our target to recruit one hundred new members, especially younger people, who can progress to become the future drivers and captains, so that the sight and sound of *President* can continue on the canals and rivers of England.

If I have tempted you, then please visit *President*'s website, http://www.nb-president.org.uk, to read reports of previous trips, look at a detailed itinerary of the year's journeys, enjoy many more photographs and, hopefully, download a membership form.

David Powell

Friends of President Committee, 1984 - 2009
Officers and Members – Past and **Present**

Peter Anthony - *chairman*
Brian Bennett - *treasurer*
John Byham - *sales*
Peter Chalk
Penny Clover - *fundraising*
Bob Crompton
Geoff Dean - *publicity - editor*
Michelle Ellison
Andrew Flack
Bill Fowler - *sponsorship - crewing*
Mike Furse - *membership*
John Goldrick
Alan Green - *chairman*
Trevor Hale - *editor*
Nick Haynes - ***membership - secretary***
Andrew Holbrook
Bob Jervis - *secretary - treasurer*
Les Langworthy - *chief engineer*
Jim Matthias - *treasurer*
Judith Matthias - *treasurer*
David McDougall - *BCM representative*
Tony Millatt - *membership - treasurer*
Ian Myers - *secretary -membership - editor*
George Naldrett - *sponsorship*
Sean Neill - *editor*
Malcolm Nixon - *treasurer - secretary - editor -* ***webmaster***
Simon Nuttall - ***treasurer*** *- secretary - editor -* ***vice chairman***
Maurice Parker
Ian Pearson
Dave Powell - ***chairman***
Richard Prince
Neil Ratcliffe - ***sales***
Keith Rogers - *editor*
Dave Speer - *editor*
Judy Spencer - *secretary*
Ron Spencer - *working parties*
Dave Stott - *minutes secretary-* ***chief engineer***
Richard Thomas - ***crewing - archivist***
David Upton
Ian Walden - ***BCLM representative***
Mike Wilkinson - *secretary*
Louise Wood - *secretary*
Nigel Wood - *editor*